D1714796

CURRICULUM STRATEGIES

CURRICULUM STRATEGIES

Social Skills Intervention for
Young African-American Males

GEORGE R. TAYLOR

Westport, Connecticut
London

MAI 385 3498

Library of Congress Cataloging-in-Publication Data

Taylor, George R.
   Curriculum strategies : social skills intervention for young
African-American males / George R. Taylor.
     p.   cm.
   Includes bibliographical references and index.
   ISBN 0–275–95200–2 (alk. paper)
    1. Social skills—Study and teaching—United States.
  2. Interpersonal relations—Study and teaching—United States.
  3. Afro-American boys—Education—United States. 4. Afro-American
young men—Education—United States. I. Title.
HQ783.T38   1997
302′.14′07—dc20   95–51428

British Library Cataloguing in Publication Data is available.

Library of Congress Catalog Card Number: 95–51428
ISBN: 0–275–95200–2

First published in 1997

Praeger Publishers, 88 Post Road West, Westport, CT 06881
An imprint of Greenwood Publishing Group, Inc.

Printed in the United States of America

The paper used in this book complies with the
Permanent Paper Standard issued by the National
Information Standards Organization (Z39.48–1984).

10 9 8 7 6 5 4 3 2 1

Contents

vi   Contents

Tables

Preface

This social skills curriculum has been developed as a guide to assist educators in instructing young African-American males how to determine what behaviors are acceptable and what behaviors are not acceptable in our society. It is also designed to assist individuals working with young African-American males. Parents and other family members will find these strategies useful for follow-up activities from the school.

Socialization skills that are assessed as necessary for young African-American males to function successfully in society are highlighted. In particular, the social skills outlined in the text stress strategies needed for: (1) respecting the rights and privacy of others; (2) learning how to handle anger; (3) learning how to act in public places; (4) showing good sportsmanship; (5) taking responsibility for one's own actions; (6) encouraging self-control; (7) selecting alternatives to using profanity; (8) learning when to apologize; (9) selecting alternatives to telling lies; and (10) dealing with individuals who hit or threaten others.

This book presumes that a basic understanding of instructional methods and procedures has been attained. Hence it does not address all of the dimensions of a functional curriculum; neither does it overview all of the possible instructional activities that can be employed in teaching social skills to young African-American males. Rather, the book provides a framework for innovative educators to extrapolate additional methods and procedures for teaching appropriate social and interpersonal skills to young African-American males.

Many of the materials contained in this book are a direct result of inservice presentations, consultancies with public schools, and empirical research projects dealing with improving social skills of young African-American males. Additional research studies are included for the reader's assessment and review.

Acknowledgments

The methods and procedures outlined in this social skills curriculum have been developed over a period of years. They were developed to address the critical issue of providing early social skills training to young African-American males. The author was of the opinion that a functional systematic approach to teaching social skills was needed in order to equip these boys for functioning successfully in society.

Compiling this textbook was not an individual endeavor. It would have been impossible to complete this awesome task without the assistance of others. A deep sense of gratitude is extended to the following schools in the Baltimore City Public School System and to my colleagues at Coppin State College in Baltimore, Maryland:

- The Sinclair Lane Elementary School and its staff.
- The Robert Coleman Elementary School and its staff.
- Robert Solomon, Division of Exceptional Children, Baltimore City Public Schools.
- Mrs. Lavania Fitzpatrick and Doctor Geraldine Waters for proofing the manuscript.
- Ms. Veronica Mack and Ms. LaVonne Stewart for the first typing of the manuscript.

A **special** thanks is given to Dr. Bernadette Francisco, Adjunct Professor of Special Education, Coppin State College, for her sincere commitment and efforts in proofing, editing and typing the final manuscript.

1

Introduction

The severity and complexity of urban education problems have become so widely publicized that they may be considered common knowledge. It is readily recognized that there are many deep-rooted problems facing the educational system today. Problems plaguing the urban schools include drugs, violence, outdated equipment, apathy, low expectations by educators and students, classism, racism, and communities that do not seem to care. Schools and school districts are ill equipped to address and resolve all the problems and challenges faced with daily (Wright, 1992).

A concerted community effort is needed to reverse the present trend. Interagency cooperation from the various human services departments is needed, headed by the school. Basic physical, social and emotional problems must be addressed, minimized, reduced, or eliminated before children can be successfully educated.

Many deprived Black male children reside in substandard environments where they are denied appropriate mental, physical and social stimulation. The culture and life styles of these communities impede normal growth and development in several key areas of functioning (Matsueda & Heines, 1987; Butler, O., 1989; Hatch & Gardner, 1988; Tomlinson, 1988). The impact of these negative cultural and life experiences have resulted in some alarming statistics.

Throughout history, many African-American males have faced adverse conditions. Wright (1992) reported that the African-American males in America continue to be that of an endangered species. It is apparent from statistical data that the African American community is in a crisis. For example, Shade and Edwards, (1987, p.123) have documented that 86% of Black youth live in poverty..., 1 out of every 22 Black American males will be killed by violent crime..., 51% of violent crime in the U.S. is committed by Black youth..., 1 out of every 6 Black males will be arrested by the time he reaches the age of 19..., 40% of Black children are being raised in "fatherless" homes. The reasons why these statistics are so high among Black males are multiple and deep rooted. Consequently, much of Chapter 1 has been devoted to addressing this issue.

Too many young African Americans become entangled in the criminal justice system due chiefly to environmental influences. Frequently, social skills, grades, education, motivation and know-how are absent. These are skills needed to help them live a law-abiding life and to bring them some measure of success and personal fulfillment. Hilliard (1988) summed up the blight of urban education in this country by stating that "nothing in school reform reports and effective research in general offers promise for the massive changes in education necessary to save the huge number of children in our systems who are at risk." He concluded that the most at risk segment of the school population is the Black male child.

Fortunately, not all young Black males exhibit the aforementioned traits. A significant percentage of young African-American males are not at risk. They live in environments that promote self-esteem and self-activity with appropriate models to emulate. The home environment provides the necessary support and love necessary for appropriate social and emotional development (Ayers, 1989; Kagan, 1989; Bradley, et al., 1989). Intervention and strategies outlined in this book are designed to improve interpersonal skills of at risk young African-American males.

A HOLISTIC APPROACH

Some young African-American males are being educated in substandard schools in most urban school districts. We have not done a satisfactory job of providing quality education for these individuals, the schools have failed to educate the "whole child." A recent report by the National Association of State Boards of Education (1992), noted that a holistic view that is attuned to the student's nonacademic needs must be included as part of his/her instructional program. This includes social, emotional, and personal citizenship training.

Instruction that minimizes the teaching of social and civic responsibility in the quest for academic excellence may not produce well-informed citizens in our society. Other researchers have voiced similar concerns (Bilken, 1990; Forest, 1990; Barth, 1990; Eisner, 1991;

Lutfiyya, 1988; O'Brien & O'Brien, 1991) in support of a holistic integrated approach to educating children. It was recommended that to avoid fragmenting school experiences, students' social and emotional well-being must be integrated and infused into a total program emphasizing social and interpersonal needs, communication needs, and academic needs. The schools must begin to use the vast amount of research present to experiment with various ways of including social skills development into the curriculum if young African-American males are to achieve their maximum potential.

The concept of teaching the whole child has been advocated since the beginning of this century. Historically, the school has mainly focused on academics, not the emotional development of children. However, a body of research draws attention to the importance of emotions in teaching children. Attention, learning, and memory are all associated with one's emotions. This concept does not appear to be readily understood by educators; thus, it is not adequately reflected in the curriculum. The school should conduct empirical studies showing the relationship between an emotionally positive classroom and the academic achievement and emotional health of pupils (Kandel & Kandel, 1994; Vincent, 1990).

The emotional system is a complex process under the direction and supervision of the brain. It is frequently viewed as a more powerful determinant of our behavior than our rational processes. Our emotional system is a complex, widely distributed, and error-prone system that defines our basic personality early in life, and is quite resistant to change. The clear implication of this research is that positive models and early interventions are needed if healthy emotions are to emerge. A detailed discussion of the emotional system is outside the scope of this text. The reader is referred to the following sources one through five.

The educational application of emotional research is still in its infancy. Since the concept is so important however, some general principles to guide classroom applications are provided:

> · We should seek to develop forms of self-control among students and staff that encourage nonjudgmental, disruptive venting of emotions.
> · Schools should focus more on metacognitive activities that encourage students to talk about their emotions and listen to their classmates' feelings.
> · Activities that emphasize social interaction and engage the entire body tend to provide the best emotional support.

· School activities that draw out emotions-simulations,
role playing, and cooperative projects—provide important contextual memory prompts.
· Emotionally stressful school environments are counter
productive because they can reduce students' ability to
learn.

Cummins, (1984) findings also supported the notion of education the
whole child based on assessment of instruction models currently used
by public schools to educate minority individuals. These models are
mostly based upon cognitive theories and include (1) analysis of
academic tasks, (2) establishment of sequential learning objectives
based on each task analysis, and (3) direct instruction of individual
task components. Most instruction and teaching in the public schools
are based on the aforementioned models (Tharp, 1989; Poplin, 1988).

African-American males have different learning styles and
frequently cannot achieve success with these traditional models; which
often do not consider the learning styles or integrated social skills
experiences needed for young African-American males to experience
school success. For example, some learners focus on global aspects of
a problem while others focus on specific points. Ideally, a student
should be flexible enough to do both. However, since schools
traditionally give more weight to analytical than to holistic approaches, the student who does not manifest analytical habits is at a decided
disadvantage (Hilliard, 1989). It is abundantly clear from the research
that schools are not attuned or designed to educate young African-
American males. Radical intervention models are needed, therefore,
that stress social skills and interpersonal skills development. The
schools cannot accomplish this awesome task alone, however, deep-
seated societal problems must be addressed concurrently with
education and educational problems, such as early environmental and
home intervention strategies.

EARLY ENVIRONMENTAL EXPERIENCES

Children born in poverty and neglect often suffer from deprivation
that seriously impairs their abilities to learn. Early prevention
programs for those at risk children and their parents (starting with
prenatal care and including health care, quality daycare, and preschool
education) help prevent debilitating later educational efforts (Butler,
1989).

A key reason why some Black and deprived children have such a
high rate of educational failure is that they often lag in physical and

psychological development and may be unprepared to meet the demands of academic learning. For example, there is evidence to support that the lack of early experiences can affect brain development. Some areas of the brain require stimulation at the right time in order to take on their normal functions. Case studies of deprived and Black children indicate that there may be critical periods for cognitive and language development (Hatch & Gardner, 1988). Therefore, intervention in the early years appears to be the most effective way to improve the prospects for deprived children to receive maximum benefits from their educational experiences.

Impoverishment of a child's early environmental experiences, including any major restrictions on play activities or lack of feedback from older individuals, is suspected of retarding his/her social development and learning. Lack of adequate adult stimulation in the early years can lead to development of negative social behavior which may be irreversible. First, in the absence of adequate stimulation and activity, neurophysiological mechanisms involved in learning may fail to develop. Second, conditions in impoverished environments, such as the slums, generally do not provide sufficient variety and duration of exposure to perceptual-motor experiences compared to more affluent environments (Dalli, 1991; Dewitt, 1994).

Children learn violent behaviors early. We need to start with the 3 year-olds and teach them more appropriate ways to handle frustration, such as, thinking about the consequences of behaviors and decisions.

HOME ENVIRONMENT

According to Butler, (1989), children born into poverty and neglect often suffer from debilitating deprivations that seriously impair their ability to learn. Hamburg (1992) indicated that early prevention programs for these at risk children and their parents reduce educational problems during the school years. Intervention in the earliest years is the most cost-effective way to improve the prospects of disadvantaged children.

Individuals are influenced by the elements within their environments. As a result, if we live in an environment that is a good match for our needs and abilities we will likely be more productive and prone to stay and will achieve academically. Individuals in mismatched environments, such as deprived Black children, often have trouble transferring values from one environment to another; therefore, many leave school when they reach the legal age. All children, including Black children, learn a great deal outside of the classroom. They have accomplished a vast amount of nonacademic

learning before they enter school and continue to learn from nonacademic sources while they are enrolled. Historically, the schools have
not tapped this great learning resource. Values, styles, and concepts
that deprived Black children bring to the schools must be matched and
integrated into their own social reality if school experiences are to be
meaningful.

Research reported by Erikson as early as 1959 supported the notion
that environments characterized by mistrust, doubt, limitations, and
feelings of inferiority and powerlessness contribute to identity
confusion and inhibit the development of the mature individual
(Erikson, 1959). In support of Eriksons view, Ayers (1989) wrote that
children need the home base of family life in order to grow up healthy
and strong. They need to be listened to and understood, nurtured, and
challenged by caring, committed adults. Parents need to contribute to
their children's self-esteem, self-activity or self-control through
appropriate modeling strategies.

If a child's early development and early home environment are both
low, there is an increased likelihood of poor developmental outcomes.
The home environment is the foundation for further development
within the child. Thus, it should be where the child receives support,
experiences love, and acquires important skills towards becoming a
productive, happy, social and emotional person. Experiences from the
home need to be integrated with the school curriculum for meaningful
experiences to occur, which will necessitate including the family and
the community in the education process (Kagan, 1989; Bradley, et al.,
1989).

Many young African-American males live in substandard environments where they are denied appropriate mental, physical, and social
stimulations. These conditions impede normal development in all
areas of functioning. Consequently, direct and immediate intervention
must be made in the social environment of these children if they are
to profit sufficiently from their school experiences.

Early Intervention Legislation

P.L. 99-457 (Part H Infants and Toddlers Program) is designed, in
part, to offset some of the deprivation discussed here by assisting
states in setting up early intervention programs for children from birth
through age 21. Early intervention services include physical, mental,
social and emotional, language and speech, and self-help skills.
Special education services may be provided to children from birth
through age 21 who have special needs, such as a physical disability,
partial or total loss of sight, severe emotional problems, hearing or
speech impairment, mental handicap, or learning disabilities. The key

is early intervention, which should be designed to treat, prevent, and reduce environmental factors associated with disabling conditions and the impediment of social growth and development.

P.L. 99-457 was greatly needed due to the public dissatisfaction with earlier legislation created for the disabled. There was also a need for early care and education not just for the disabled child, but for the healthy child. Two factors contributed to the search for early childcare services: (1) the increase in the number of mothers who were working outside the home, and (2) the realization that many of these children were disadvantaged or from culturally different families and often not developmentally ready for school (Gallagher, 1989).

Kagan (1989) supported the issues addressed in P.L. 99-457, and further argued the importance of having early care and education of children go beyond the school doors. Again, emphasis was placed on including the family and the community in the educational process of children. Kagan's arguments for including the family and community stem from the realization that children are coming from more fragmented families, yet the technological advances of today's society require more complex environments. As a result, it is now more important than ever that the child is building on one stage of development to another by accomplishing certain learning tasks and by proceeding from the simple task to the more complex.

TRANSFORMING THE ENVIRONMENT

A major factor affecting how well we function in our environment is self-esteem. Promoting self-esteem among children assists in reducing problems that otherwise may surface later in life. Several authorities have advocated the need for additional research in this area to evaluate the impact of strategies and programs designed to promote self-esteem (Butler, O., 1989; Myers, 1990).

Although we still need empirical data on the effectiveness of programs to raise self-esteem among children, high self-esteem appears to promote confidence, security, citizenship, and academic success. Recommended strategies or principles for improving self-concepts include:

- Praise rather than criticize.
- Teach children to set achievable goals.
- Teach children to praise themselves and to capitalize on their strong points.
- Teach children to praise others.
- Set realistic expectation levels.

- Teach children to have confidence in themselves.
- Praise children for achieving or failing after at tempting to achieve.
- Praise children for successfully completing a test or project.
- Praise children for positive criticism.
- Accept pupils' contributions without judgment.
- Listen to children; they have important information to share.
- Maintain a "you can do it" philosophy.
- Present challenges for children.
- Provide movement and freedom within the classroom for children to achieve objectives.
- Show concern and warmth.
- Set high classroom control rules with input from children.
- Demonstrate and show respect for children.
- Provide an atmosphere for success.
- Listen to how you talk to children.
- Catch someone doing something right and tell him/her about it.
- Attack the behavior, not the student; separate the behavior from the child.
- Use modeling or other techniques to reduce mal adaptive behavior.
- Teach children to respect themselves and others.
- Teach children to be proud of their heritage.
- Provide activities that incorporate parental involve ment.

These strategies are not conclusive and should be expanded as assessed by the teachers.

ENHANCING SELF-ESTEEM OF YOUNG AFRICAN-AMERICAN MALES

Due to various factors within society and the community, the schools' role in enhancing self-esteem is of prime importance. Intervention must be made early to break or prevent failure due to low self-esteem. Thus, there appears to be a positive relationship between self-concept and student's success or failure in school (Taylor, 1993).

Many factors influence the young African-American male's development prior to going to school. When the school accepts the child, it should be committed to accepting and attempting to teach the whole child, not just developing the three R's. A major factor in children's development in the beginning school years is the view of themselves as they communicate with other students. For young African-American males, as well as other students, self-concept influences the motivation to learn. If students do not feel good about themselves generally, and good about themselves specifically as learners, they will lack the motivation to improve their performance in many academic areas. Group and individual activities are needed in order to improve the self-concepts of young African-American males. Specific activities have been developed to improve self-concepts in Chapter 8.

The role of the teacher in promoting self-control cannot be overemphasized. Specifically, the teacher exerts considerable influence on a child's self-concept through the types of treatment, beliefs, and expectations that are upon the child. Children quickly react to an interpret negative traits projected by the teacher. The child's interpretation of the teacher's actions and their significance plays an important role in how the child reacts.

Children sift, seek, reject, and avoid information from individuals they do not respect or trust. Thus, they do not accept information from adults who have rejected them as readily as they do from adults who they feel have accepted them and seem trustworthy. Teachers can exert significant influence on the forming of the child's self-concept by constructing nurturing and positive learning environments, as well as showing positive attitudes and developing rapport with children.

Children's socioeconomic status should have no affect on how teachers judge their ability to learn. Teachers who classify children into social class memberships tend to show their prejudices toward selected groups of children. One major condition for enhancing self-esteem in the classroom is the teacher's acceptance of the child. By accepting the child, the teacher indicates to the child that he/she is worthy of his/her attention and respect.

Another condition that promotes self-esteem is the presence of explicit limits in the classroom that are spelled out early and are consistently enforced. Such limits should involve input from the children. They should define acceptable behavior, provide standards of conduct, and establish behavior expectations in the classroom and school. Standards and regulations are necessary for children to develop positive self-esteem because they set limits and expectations.

A child's personality is organized around various aspects of self-awareness and self-concept. The structure of the school and the teachers' behavior greatly impact personality development. What we believe about ourselves affects what we do, what we see and hear, and our ability to cope in the environment. That is, self-concept is significantly influenced by life experiences due chiefly to the fact that it is learned, much of it through modeling. Young African-American males who have Black male teachers have better self-concepts than boys who have female teachers (Mancus, 1992; Ingrassia, 1993; Lapoint, 1992). Collectively, these studies suggest that the presence of Black teachers in the classroom provides a positive role model for the boys to emulate.

McRay's study (1994) supported the above premise. In a study involving young African-American males, he sampled both white and Black teachers' opinions of whether or not race made a difference in teaching young African-American boys. Seventy-two percent of the subjects responded that race made a difference in teaching young African-American males.

It is the view of this author that Black role models for young African-American males to emulate are very important; however, they should not be the sole criterion for predicting or determining success. Further, teachers who have a genuine interest in these boys, and who provide stimulating learning experiences, regardless of race or sex, can and will promote positive self-concepts. The key ingredient appears to be early intervention to compensate for negative early experiences. Many of the early life experiences of young African-American male children are negative and fail to provide opportunity for the self to emerge successfully. Consequently, many of these boys' self-concepts are lower than those of their healthy peers. By the time many young African-American males attend school, their attitudes toward school is well entrenched. Unfortunately, many of these attitudes are negative.

If these boys are to achieve successful academic progress, the school must develop interpersonal and social skills strategies that enable them to feel better about themselves. In some instances, social skills should supersede academic skills. Appropriate social skills must be taught and modeled for many of these children before a meaningful academic program can be pursued.

Not only are social skills important in academic areas; they are also related to socialization. Several behaviors are necessary in the socialization process, including the emergence of self-identity and self-concept. While social skills are developed through interactions with family, school, and the community, nothing is as important as the role of the parents. Parents provide the model for self-acceptance and the feeling that life is worthwhile. Also, parents who demonstrate a positive self-concept and high self-esteem treat their children with respect and acceptance and provide them with support and encouragement.

A child's social skills are shaped by the reinforcement he or she receives as a result of an action in the environment (Wood, 1984). Lack of social development diminishes the social status within the group (Anita & Kreimeyer, 1992; Odom & McEvoy, 1988; Peck & Cooke, 1983). Environmental conditions that nurture negative and aggressive behaviors must be transformed. To this end massive financial, social, and psychological support must be provided early. A coordinated community effort is needed to offset the present conditions in many urban communities in this country.

SUMMARY

Individuals are products of their environments. They imitate experiences to which they have been exposed. Personality is conceived as a product of social learning. Its development is largely a function of the social conditions under which one grows up. There is frequently a conflict between these children's social values and the expectations of the school. This is chiefly due to the school not being tolerant of the cultural and behavioral styles of young African-American male children. Appropriate social skills should be taught and modeled for them before a meaningful academic program can be pursued. Since many of the habits developed by African-American males are well entrenched by the time they enter school, surface attention will not have a significant impact on changing negative habits. Instead, a coordinated and integrated program is needed. This book was designed to accomplish such a purpose. Actual classroom practices based upon fieldtesting are stressed throughout the book.

REFERENCES

Gazzaniga, M. (1989). *Mind matters: How did mind and brain interact to create our conscious lives.* Boston: Houghton-Mifflin.

Kandel, M. & Kandel, E. (1994). Flights of memory. *Discover Magazine*, 32-38.

Levinthal, C. (1988). *Messengers of paradise: Opiates and the brain.* New York: Double Day.

Moyer, B. (1992). *Healing and the mind.* New York: Double Day.

Vincent, J.P. (1990). *The biology of emotions.* Cambridge, MA.: Basil Blackwell.

2

Social Learning Theories: An Overview

During the last two decades we have witnessed the rediscovery, creation, or validation of a diversity of social learning theories. These theories have provided us with a common language with which we can communicate about the affects of social learning theories of academic performance of minority and deprived children.

The study of social learning theories enables the school to better understand both how young African-American male children think about school-related processes and how they likely feel about themselves in relation to the process. The school's understanding of both the cognitive and the affective characteristics of deprived children may be termed "empathic." One way of showing empathy to children is by designing effective classroom environments that consider the cognitive and affect levels of the children (Butler, 1988; Hilliard, 1989).

THEORETICAL FRAMEWORK

The major emphasis of social learning theories is on environmental learner interaction. The learning of behaviors that are socially accepted, as well as those that are not, is "social learning." This view is supported by Stuart (1989) who maintained that social learning theories attempt to describe the process by which we come to know what behaviors should or should not be projected when we are in different types of social situations.

The theories themselves are learning theories that have been applied to social situations. Generally, therefore, they have been behavioristic rather than cognitive (Bandura, 1977). These theories do not separate the parts from the whole; instead, they have as a major underlying concept the holistic and interactive nature of development. For example, the various areas of the self do not exist or develop separately from one another, and movement toward maturity in one area can affect movement and learning in another area. Social learning theories also address individual differences and how such factors as personality temperament and sociological influences may interact with the developmental process.

Learning theories assist us in identifying how different individuals may manage, delay, progress through, or retreat from developmental tasks. These theories also suggest that there are persistent individual differences such as cognitive style, temperament, or ethnic background that interact with development. Additionally, these theories provide knowledge about individual types and styles that may be critical to our understanding of differing sources of reward and punishment for students (Stuart, 1989).

VYGOTSKY'S THEORY

Vygotsky's theory, according to Moll (1991), lends support to the concept that natural properties as well as social relations and constraints make possible the social construction of a child's higher psychological processes. The three major components of Vygotskian theory are: (1) the internalization of auxiliary culture means; (2) the interpersonal, or social process of mediation; (3) a child's knowledge is formed within the zone of proximal development, a cognitive space defined by social relational boundaries.

One of the major tenets of Vygotsky's theory (Moll, 1991) is that there is a functional relationship between the effects of the culture on cognitive development and biological growth. Whereas the physical, biological, and neurological determinants are more readily understood and agreed upon, the impact of the cultural determinants is not as easily understood. Cultural determinants include social processes which transform naturally through the mastery and use of culture signs. In essence, the natural development of children's behavior forms the biological conditions necessary to develop higher psychological processes. Culture, in turn, provides the conditions by which the higher psychological processes may be realized.

COMMONALITY AMONG THEORIES

The common threads uniting these theories and concepts are *imitation, modeling,* and *copying behaviors* (Bandura & Walters, 1963). As do all children, young African-American males imitate, model, and copy behaviors directly from their environments. Recently, these models have become inappropriate and often create conflict and tension between children, society, and the school. Therefore, learning, culture, and behavioral styles of African-American males should be, as much as possible, incorporated and integrated into a total learning packet. Social learning theories provide a concrete framework for society and schools to begin implementing additional social skills strategies into the curriculum.

"Social skills" is a term used to describe a wide range of behaviors varying in complexity and is thought to be necessary for effective social functioning and academic success (Obiakor, 1990, 1991, 1992). Behaviors that constitute social skills development may vary depending upon the situation, role, sec, age, and disabling conditions.

INTEGRATIVE ASPECTS OF SOCIAL SKILLS DEVELOPMENT

As indicated throughout this text, one of the major reasons why young African-American males' behaviors are frequently rejected by schools and social institutions may be attributed to young African-American males failure to display appropriate social skills needed for different social interactions.

Various types of social skills instruction must be developed and systematically taught to young African-American males. The earlier the intervention, the sooner negative behaviors can be addressed. As indicated in Chapter 1, both the home and the school should play dominant roles in developing pro-social skills due to several factors associated within the urban environment.

The school may be the most appropriate agency, along with parental input, to conduct the social skills training or intervention. Teaching students pro-social skills necessary to cope with the social demands of society creates a climate in which positive relationships can exist and where students can be empowered to direct their own successes. A safe, supportive environment tends to facilitate learning. Pro-social skills taught and practiced daily in a nurturing environment assist in reducing negative behavior and in promoting positive ones (Taylor, 1992).

Social skills are developed through interactions with family, school, and community, and are shaped by reinforcement received as a result of such interactions. Often children do not learn effectively from past experiences. Frequently, they are enabled to transfer one socially accepted behavior to another social situation, thus their behaviors are frequently interpreted as immature, inept, or intrusive. This negative feedback prohibits future social interactions. This is especially true for young African-American males.

Research findings suggest a significant relationship between social skills intervention and academic achievement. Thus, many social skill procedures, such as attending and positive interaction techniques, have been shown to increase academic performance. According to Oswald and Sinah-Nirbhay (1992), social skills interventions appear to work best when they correspond to actual interactions in the naturalistic environment. Similar findings by Walker, Irvin, Noell, and Singer (1992), indicated that some individuals do not have sufficient social skills to be successful in school. Finally, Walker (1992) stressed that there is an urgent need for social skills training that is integrated into the curriculum.

Lack of appropriate social training may not permit many young African-American males to engage productively in social events. Special techniques and intervention related to remediating poor or inappropriate skills must be addressed early in their school experiences in order to bring their social skills up to acceptable school standards. According to Holland (1987) and Ayers (1989), early intervention is needed to expose young Black males to appropriate social models.

For many, their culture experiences have not provided appropriate social skills for them to be successful in the larger community or cope with appropriate social behavior. The same applies to young African-American males. Changing inappropriate social behavior involves infusing principles of social learning theories such as modeling, imitation, and behavioral techniques with social skills instruction. Once social skills deficits have been identified, the social learning principles may be used to reinforce or reward appropriate social behavior.

SOCIAL SKILLS MODELS OF YOUNG
AFRICAN-AMERICAN MALES

Research findings have demonstrated that diverse groups of children, such as young Black males, are at risk for developing inappropriate interpersonal skills. Thus, social skills deficiencies are commonly observed in this population. Several factors may attribute to these deficiencies such as child-rearing practices, deprived cultural environments, and lack of understanding of social expectations or rules.   In turn, such deficiencies may lead to inappropriate or inadequate social behaviors.

Since social skills are learned throughout a lifetime from imitating or modeling both negative and positive behaviors, many individuals lack basic interpersonal skills if deprived of appropriate models. These individuals are frequently at a disadvantage in society and tend to feel inadequate and use unproductive and unacceptable ways of relating and communicating with others.

The importance of interpersonal skills instruction has been mini-mized in the schools.   Mastering these skills requires training and practice.   Interpersonal skills training allows children to recognize appropriate social behaviors, understand individuals' responses to certain behaviors, and respond appropriately.   Lack of these skills often leads to feelings of rejection and isolation in a classroom or any public setting.

Beyond the areas discussed here, there is also ample evidence to suggest that children's social difficulties may emanate from different sources and areas.   Such areas must be identified and remediated during the early years.   Schools must design direct and immediate intervention programs that will permit young Black males to experi-ence success (Butler, 1988; Hilliard, 1989; Kagan, 1989; Bradley, et al, 1989; Diggory, 1990; Foster, 1986; Deal, 1990; Holland, 1987; Ayers, 1989).

ANGER AND HOSTILITY

Studies have consistently shown that negative behaviors such as anger and hostility are learned behaviors that children imitate from their environments.   These behaviors manifest themselves in hostile and destructive patterns of behavior, which frequently cannot be controlled by the schools, thus creating conflict and tension between children, parents, and the schools (Matsueda & Heimer, 19887; Gibbs, 1988).

Constructively expressing anger and hostility requires a great deal of inner control.   Internal awareness of anger must first be established. If one is not aware of anger, it cannot be controlled.   When anger is repressed or ignored, it will surface later and add to one's frustration. Further, usually by that time, anger is expressed in aggressive behaviors such as attempts to harm someone, destroy something, make insults, and through hostile statements and actions.   Aggressive behaviors manifest themselves in ways that infringe upon the rights of others.

Controlling anger and managing feeling are essential in developing appropriate interpersonal skills. Children should be taught how to control anger through application of the following:

1. Recognizing and describing anger.
2. Finding appropriate ways to express anger.
3. Analyzing and understanding factors responsible for anger.
4. Managing anger by looking at events differently or talking oneself out of anger.
5. Learning how to repress feelings.
6. Expressing anger constructively.
7. Experimenting with alternative ways of expressing anger.

A variety of strategies may be used to assist pupils in controlling or reducing anger. Role playing, creative dramatics, physical activities, timeout, relaxation therapy, writing and talking out feelings, assertive behavioral techniques, managing provocations, and resolving interpersonal conflicts through cooperative approaches are but a few techniques that teachers may employ.

Teaching Apology Strategies

Apologies can restore relationships, heal humiliations, and generate forgiveness, if taught appropriately. It is a powerful social skill, but is generally not considered to be important by the school. It may be concluded, therefore, that the school views it to be a function of the home. However, as reflected throughout this book, the school must assume the leadership in teaching all social skills. This is especially true for a significant number of young African-American males, many of whom consider apologies to be signs of weaknesses, to display feminine traits, and admit failure. The few research studies reported indicate the reverse: Apologies require great strength, empathy, security and strength (Taylor, 1992).

Failure to apologize can stain relationships, create grudges, and instill bitter vengeances. As mentioned, apologies are a show of strength because not only do they restore the self-concepts of those offended, they make us more sensitive to the feelings and needs of others. Like all social skills, appropriate ways to apologize must be taught.

Specific strategies have been outlined for teaching most social skills to young African-American males in Chapter 8. Anger and hostility and the need to teach apology strategies have been observed and associated with many of the poor social skills shown by some young African-American males.

Harris (1992) concluded that many African-American males may have developed or adapted alternative ways and styles of coping with problems in their neighborhoods. These behavioral styles are frequently in conflict with the school and society in general, and may be viewed as negative or destructive. Behavioral styles and models copied and imitated by young African-American males may serve them well in their environments, but are frequently viewed as dysfunctional by the school and society.

The ability of low-achieving young African-American males to function satisfactorily in social groups and to maintain dispositions, habits, and attitudes customarily associated with character and personality is usually below levels set by the school. Thus, they are more likely than other children to be rejected by their peers, demonstrate fewer less rigid controls over their impulses, display learned hostile and destructive patterns of behavior, and often seem unable to respond to traditional classroom instruction.

TEACHING SELF-REGULATION SKILLS

Instructional programs must be developed and designed to enable young African-American males to gain knowledge about appropriate interpersonal skills and to employ this newly acquired knowledge in solving their social problems. For this goal to be accomplished, these boys must be taught effective ways of internalizing their behaviors and assessing how their behaviors affect others. Helping young African-American males develop self-regulation skills appears to be an excellent technique for bringing behaviors to the conscious level where they can be controlled. Some of the more commonly used self-regulation skills are summarized in the following.

Be Aware of One's Thinking Patterns

Provide "think-aloud" activities and model how to solve problems by working through tasks and asking questions such as (1) What is needed to solve the problem? (2) Things are not working out, should I try another way? and (3) What assistance do I need to solve the problem?

As teachers perform these think-aloud activities, they may ask for input from the student relevant to the type of self-regulation skills being demonstrated. Skills may have to be modeled and demonstrated several times. Provide opportunities for the boys to demonstrate them individually and in cooperative groups, as well as to evaluate the effectiveness of their actions.

Making A Plan

Have the boys identify specific examples where self-regulation is useful. Motivation may come from a story, file, tape, or creative dramatic activities. Instruct the boys to develop a plan to reduce, correct, or eliminate the undesirable behaviors. As the boys demonstrate the behaviors, the teacher should reinforce and praise them.

Develop and Evaluate Long-Term Goals

Employ self-regulation strategies to assist the boys in accomplishing long-term goals. First have the boys identify social and behavioral goals. Record these goals and assist the boys in making a plan, as outlined previously. Schedule a time to meet with the boys to determine how well the goals are being achieved. In some instances, the goals will need to be modified or adapted such that they focus on specific behaviors. Self-regulation strategies make actions more controllable by making us aware of our own behavior. Once awareness is achieved, the plan outlined earlier may be taught to bring behaviors under control.

A variety of techniques and strategies may be used in developing self-regulation skills: (1) Role playing; (2) Classifying behaviors and identifying types of self-regulation strategies to employ; (3) Working in cooperative groups; (4) Positively reinforcing the mental habits; (5) Reading and developing stories; (6) Being sensitive to feedback and criticism; (7) Teaching self-monitoring skills; (8) Seeking outside advice when needed; and (9) Evaluating progress.

Self-regulation is one of several strategies that may be used to teach appropriate social skills to young African-American males. Appropriate social skills are essential for developing personal relationships and accepting the roles of authority figures. Since social behaviors are learned, they can be changed and modified with appropriate intervention. They require that an individual evaluate the situation, choose the appropriate skills, and perform the social tasks appropriately (Katz, 1991). Unfortunately, many young African-American males have not been exposed to appropriate social models or do not possess enough prerequisite skills, such as maturity and self-control, to successfully perform the social skills. As mentioned, development of social skills in African-American males, as well as in all children, requires that they have appropriate models to copy and imitate, that they can recognize non-verbal clues, and that they adjust their behaviors accordingly.

The research of Matsueda and Heimer (1987) and Gibbs (1988) supports the findings of Katz (1991). These authors indicated that negative behaviors are learned behaviors which children imitate from their environments. The schools view these behaviors as hostile and destructive and respond in a negative fashion, thus creating conflict and tension between schools and children.

Several researches (Hilliard, 1989; Deal, 1990; Bilken, 1990; Taylor, 1992; Forest, 1990; Collins and Hatch, 1992; Kagan, 1980; Johnson & Johnson, 1990) have directly implied that social skills must be taught and integrated into the curriculum and assume a position of primacy along with the basic three R's.

Findings from other studies support these studies by concluding that many African-American males may have developed or adapted alternative ways and styles of coping with problems within their communities, which are frequently in conflict with the school and society in general and, therefore are viewed as negative or destructive (Harris, 1992; Taylor, 1992; Hilliard, 1989).

SUMMARY

Social learning theories offer the school a common context through which young African-American males' environment, developmental sequence, and early experiences can be understood and researched. Thus, these theories enable educators to better understand how young African-American males think and feel about themselves, thereby making them aware of factors in the environment that precipitate cognitive and affective problems that may have some bearing on academic performance.

The relationship between social learning theories and academic performance is not well established. Most research reported today simply indicates a causal relationship. There is a dire need to conduct empirical studies to determine to what degree social learning theories impact on academic performance.

Social development is a major area in which many young African-American males need assistance, since they frequently have developed inappropriate interpersonal skills that are not accepted by the school. Inability to conform to expected social standards may result in unacceptable social skills, which are essential for developing personal relationships and accepting the role of authority figures (Taylor, 1992). Research findings by Bradley et al. (1989), Hilliard (1989), Butler (1989), Holland (1987), and Johnson and Johnson (1990) support the notion that unacceptable social behaviors are directly associated with deprived cultural environments. Innovative ways must be found to provide appropriate role models for young African-American males to imitate and copy.

3

Behavioral Styles of Young African-American Males

As indicated earlier, many young African-American males have not mastered the social skills needed to be successful at school and within the larger community, resulting in frequent conflicts between the children and school on what is considered appropriate behavior. Much of this confusion can be attributed to the school's failure to understand the impact of various cultural styles on learning. Cultural values influence the behavior of individuals. For example, young African-American males' cultural groups.

The powerful influence on cultural systems on cognitive style and behavior must be recognized and integrated into the instructional program of young African-American males (Hilliard, 1989). Curriculum planners must recognize that no one behavioral instructional strategy is appropriate for intervention. Rather, strategies should be selected based upon children's abilities and assessed needs as discussed in Chapter 4.

Some of the learning preferences found to be characteristic of African-American learners include: (1) emphasize group cooperation; (2) value harmony with nature; (3) accept affective expression; (4) tend to be holistic or Gestalt thinkers; (5) perceive the field as responding to the person and as possibly having a life of its own; (6) use strong, colorful expressions; (7) require that relevant concepts have special or personal relevance; (8) use language that is dependent upon unique context and many interactional characteristics of the communicants--time and place, on inflection, muscular movements, and nonverbal cues; (9) prefer learning material that has a human, social content and is characterized by fantasy and humor; and (10) perceived conceptual distances between the observer and the observed (Hilliard, 1989).

Consideration should be given to these characteristics when planning instructional programs for young African-American males. Each cultural style is different; however, similar characteristics operate across specific cultures. It is of prime importance that young African-American males be made aware of their cultural styles and how these impact and influence their learning. All curricula should reflect the richness and contribution of each culture.

The public schools should play a dominant role in multicultural education by including the contributions of diverse cultures. Historically, this has not been the case. Instead, it was believed there was one dominant culture in this country, based upon the mores of Northern Europe. On this premise, minorities had to assimilate into the culture the best way they could. In the latter part of this century, culture views changed, however. Advocates advanced and supported the notion that all cultures had significant contributions to make to our society. Strength in diversity was recognized. The school became the ideal social institution to advance the concept of diversity.

Through the introduction of multicultural education in the curriculum, young African-American males' self-perception will be enhanced and some of the stereotyping relevant to minorities and Blacks will be dispelled. As the self-images and concepts of young African-American males improve, they will have a source of identity and will gain excellent role models.

THE EFFECTS OF BEHAVIORAL STYLES

Style is learned; learned patterns can be either changed or augmented, but cannot be ignored. Style tends to be rooted at a deep cultural level and is largely determined by prior experiences and motivation. Hilliard's research indicated that educational dialogue in recent years has given substantial attention to the importance and precise meaning of style in teaching and learning, particularly for minority groups. Thus, style differences between teachers and students and between students and the curriculum have been cited as explanations for the low academic performance of some minority groups (Hilliard, 1989).

Misunderstanding of behavioral style can lead to misjudging students' language abilities and intelligence and can impair rapport and communication skills. Style is directly associated with cultural values and has been changed over time. Modifying style is a slow and arduous process, however, and may never be fully realized.

Proper sensitivity to style can provide a perspective for enriching instruction of all children and for improving both teacher-student communication and the systematic assessment of students. The schools must become more sensitive to style out of basic respect for children and their tremendous potential for learning (Hilliard, 1989). Additionally, a person can use more than one style and can be taught to switch styles when appropriate. According to Deal (1990), the core problems of our schools today is not technical but spiritual and social. A climate for growth depends upon healthy, fertile social relationships where the styles and experiences of African-American children are recognized. The notion that each culture has made significant contributions to mankind should be highlighted and integrated into the curriculum (Bennet, 1988; Bank, 1991; Obiakor, 1992).

CORRELATING SCHOOL ACTIVITIES TO STUDENT'S BACKGROUND AND ABILITY

Upon entering school, children are regimented and required to follow specific rules that often conflict with their styles and modes of learning. Diggory (1990) further pointed out that the child and the school conceive of learning differently. The school is mostly concerned with verbal and written expressions and standardized test results. Many of these activities are foreign to children many of whom have not developed sufficient background or skills to master them. Behavior problems frequently occur due to differences between the child's ability and the expectations imposed by the school. If the school is to be successful in meeting the needs of children, especially those from diverse backgrounds, children must be given an active role in their own learning by structuring activities that are relevant and meaningful to them. Additionally, teachers must be free to experiment with various models of instruction (Taylor, 1992).

The role of the school should not be to fill children with information, but to help them construct understanding about what they are doing. Children's competence, their ability to make meaning from their environments, to construct knowledge to form generalizations, to solve problems, and to associate and transfer knowledge is seldom encouraged by the school.

The notion that style requires a specific pedagogical response, especially at the point of applying special teaching strategies, appears to be sound. It is widely believed that such an approach ought to be attempted and that teaching and learning will be more successful as a result. Students' cultural and learning styles appear to be inseparable; therefore, matching them with appropriate instruction appears to be a sound instructional strategy.

LEARNING STYLES

Children receive and order information in different ways through a variety of dimensions and channels. Diggory (1990) implied that the school is not sensitive tot he personal learning styles pupils have developed and mastered during the developmental stages. Making sense out of the world is a very real and active process. During early childhood, children master complex tasks according to their own schedules without formal training or intervention; the structured environment of the school appears to impede the personal learning styles of many children.

While there is no one common definition of learning styles, researchers have considered learning styles from four dimensions: cognitive, affective, physiological, and psychological.

Cognitive Dimension

The cognitive dimension of learning style refers to the different ways that children mentally perceive and order information and ideas. Witken (1975) analyzed cognitive style and determined how one's perception was related to information processing. A significant relationship was noted between abstract and concrete learners style of learning.

Affective Dimension

The affective dimension refers to how students' personality traits—both social and emotional—affect their learning. This dimension refers to how the student feels about himself/herself. What way can be found to build his/her self-esteem (Butler, 1988)? Learning styles are functions of both nature and nurture and, according to Myers (1990), type development starts at a very early age. The hypothesis is that type is inborn, an innate predisposition like right- or left-handedness, but that the development of type can be greatly assisted or retarded by the environment.

Physiological Dimension

The physiological dimension of learning involves the interaction between the senses and the environment. Reynolds & Gerstein (1992) classified several channels under the physiological dimension, including (1) visual/auditory, (2) tactile/kinesthetic, and (3) a mixed combination of the five senses. The physiological dimension probes such questions as: Does the student learn better through auditory/visual or tactile/kinesthetic means? And how is the student affected by such factors as light, temperature, and room design? The physiological dimension involves the student's inner strengths and individuality.

Boys and girls process information through the physical channels differently. Specifically, prior to age 16, girls tended to have lower visual-spatial development and their brain developed earlier. Also, 10-12-year-old girls had twice the head growth of boys the same age, with boys catching up by the time they were 14 to 16. Also, girls were more sophisticated in language acts than boys of the same age. Thus, sex and individual preferences play dominant roles in grasping and transferring knowledge.

Gregorc (1993) saw style as a way of viewing the world; a way of defining the mind's goals, content and cycles, and its differentiated mediation abilities of space and time. The mind's differentiated mediation abilities divide learning styles into sets that define one's reality base and ordering trends. According to Gregorc (1993), descriptors for the various learning styles include:

    · Concrete Sequential—patient realist, instinctive, methodical.
    · Abstract Sequential—serious, intellectual realist, logical, and analytical.
    · Abstract Random—emotional idealist, perceptive.
    · Concrete Random—inquisitive, independent realist/idealist, impulsive.

Research findings strongly suggest that the dominant qualities of a learner's style are unchangeable (Guild, 1994). However, teachers can help learners be successful if they recognize their own style and use their strengths to teach toward their students' styles (Owens, 1991). Flexibility in working in the context of many styles within the classroom allows the teacher the opportunity to reach a variety of children with different learning styles. The benefits of such flexibility is immeasurable.

Finally, the issue of nature vs. nurture controversy has surfaced in the study of learning styles. Unlike Myers (1990), some researches promote the impact of environment, others promote the impact of heredity, while many are neutral. There are advantages to using all approaches. The salient point is to keep the individual needs in mind as well as the modality favored.

EVALUATING LEARNING STYLES

Pupils learn through a variety of sensory channels and demonstrate individual patterns of sensory strengths and weaknesses. Teachers should capitalize on students' learning styles in their academic programs. Several aspects are recommended when considering factors that characterize a pupil's learning style:

1. The speed at which a pupil learns is an important aspect to consider. Learning rate is not as obvious as it may appear. Frequently, a learner's characteristics interfere with his/her natural learning rate. Although the learning rate is more observable than other characteristics, it does not necessarily relate to the quality of a learner's performance. Therefore, it is of prime importance for the teacher to know as much as possible about all of a learner's characteristics.

2. The techniques the pupils use to organize materials they plan to learn also need to be considered. Individuals organize materials they expect to learn information from by remembering the broad ideas. These broad ideas trigger the details in the pupils' memory. This method of proceeding from the general to the specific is referred as *deductive style* of organization. This principle may be applied successfully in many situations.

Other pupils prefer to remember the smaller components, which then remind them of the broader concept, *inductive style* of organization. In utilizing inductive organization, the pupil may look at several items or objectives and form specific characteristics, develop general principles or concepts. Knowing a pupil's style of organization can assist the teacher in effectively guiding the learning process by presenting materials as close as possible to the student's preferred style of organization.

3. The pupil's need for reinforcement and structure in the learning situation is also important. All learners need some structure and reinforcement to their learning. This process may be facilitated through a pupil's preferred channels of input and output.

4. Input involves using the five sensory channels—auditory, visual, tactile, and kinesthetic, olfactory and gustatory—which are transmitted to the brain. In the brain, the sensory stimuli are organized into cognitive patterns and the input channel through which the person readily processes stimuli is referred to as his/her *preferred mode* or *modality*.

5. Similar differences are evident in output, which may be expressed verbally or nonverbally. Verbal output uses the fine-motor activity of the speech mechanism to express oral language. Nonverbal output uses both fine- and gross-motor activities. Fine-motor skills

may include gesture and demonstration. Pupils usually prefer to express themselves through one of these channels.

      6. A pupil's preferred model of input is not necessarily his/her strongest acuity channel. Sometimes a pupil transfers information received through one channel into another with which he/she is more comfortable. This process is called *intermodal transfer.* Pupils differ in their ability to perform the intermodal transfer. Failure to perform this task effectively may impede learning.

      The differences in learning styles and patterns of some pupils almost ensure rewarding educational achievement for successful completion of tasks. Unfortunately, this is not true for many young African-American males. The differences reflected in learning can interfere with the pupil's achievement. Early identification, assessment, and management of a pupil's learning differences can prevent more serious learning problems from occurring.

      Some children are concrete learners while others are abstract learners. Some focus on global aspects of a problem, others on specific points. Ideally, a student should be flexible enough to do both. Since schools traditionally give more weight to analytical than to holistic approaches, the student who does not manifest analytical habits is at a decided disadvantage (Hilliard, 1989).

      Assessment of a pupil's preferred mode of input and output may be conducted through formal and informal techniques. A commonly used instrument is The Learning Channel Preference Checklist. This checklist along with two other instruments will be presented here.

The Learning Channel Preference Checklist

      The Learning Channel Preference Checklist is designed for assessing learning styles. Teachers can administer the checklist and follow-up with interpretive discussions.

      Students are asked to rank each statement as it relates to them. There are no right or wrong answers. Students rate each item as often (3), sometimes (2), and never (1), on three broad categories: visual, auditory, and haptic. The highest score indicates the preferred learning style in the aforementioned categories.

      Auditory Learning Style. This is the least developed learning channel for all children, including most young African-American males.

      Visual Learning Style. Many children learn best when they can see information. High scores in this area denote that they prefer text-books over lectures and rely on lists, graphs, charts, pictures, notes, and taking notes. A significantly higher number of children rate this area higher than the auditory channel.

Haptic Learning Style. This is the most frequently reported learning channel by children. That is, most children prefer this style. Haptic students show a cluster of right-brain characteristics. They learn best from experimenting rather than from textbooks.

The combined scores in the three areas usually range from 10 to 30. Often, two areas are close. Scores in the high 20s indicate that the student has satisfactorily developed all three channels and is able to use the modality that best fits the task. Scores below 20 indicate that the student has not yet developed a strong learning channel preference.

Usually, students scoring in the 20s have great difficulty with school because they do not have a clearly defined method for processing information. These students should be treated as haptic learners because the haptic style is much easier to develop than the others.

The checklist is a diagnostic tool, which indicates areas of strengths and weaknesses in sensory acuity. Based on this information, teachers can adapt or modify the instructional program to include activities that support the strongest modality. Information from the checklist should be shared with the student. O'Brien (1989) believed that all students can benefit from knowing their learning styles, as well as how to use and manipulate them in the learning process.

The Gregorc Delineator

Another instrument that deals specifically with learning style analysis is the Gregorc Style Delineator (GSD), which uses a four-channel approach to assess personality traits. The reliability and validity of the Gregorc Style Delineator in its present form can be characterized as strong. The manual carefully points out proper usage and cautions using the instrument in minority settings. When using the instrument in minority settings, it is recommended that one be sensitive to the cultural background of subjects. Thus, it is recommended that the reader carefully review the manual and consult expert opinion before using this instrument with minority individuals.

The Myers-Briggs Type Indicator

Another well-known instrument for assessing learning styles is the Myers-Briggs Type Indicator. The instrument assesses auditory, visual, and tactile acuity by asking individuals to repeat patterns using the above modalities. Results also show differences in cognitive strengths, such as holistic and global learning, in contrast to analytic, part-to-whole approaches (Guild, 1994).

These tests are culture and language specific. Individuals respond to and interpret self-reporting instruments based on their culture experiences. These responses may be in conflict with established norms and, therefore, yield conflicting results. Consequently, caution is needed when interpreting results from minority individuals, especially young African-American males.

THE RELATIONSHIP BETWEEN CULTURE AND LEARNING STYLE

Individuals from certain cultures show a preference for certain learning styles, and this preference may affect classroom performance. Schools must recognize, therefore, that students with diverse backgrounds have a favored learning style that may affect their academic performance. When teachers fail to accommodate students' favored learning style in their instructional delivery, they may not meet students' individual needs (Guild, 1994).

Hilliard (1989) supported the above analysis when he suggested that failure to match cultural and learning styles in teaching younger students is the explanation for the low performance of many culturally different minority-group students. He contended that children, regardless of their styles, are failing primarily because of systematic inequities in the delivery of whatever pedagogical approach the teachers claim to master—not because students cannot learn from teachers whose styles do not match their own.

Guild (1994) provided three cautions when attempting to match learning styles with cultural styles:

1. Care should be taken when matching learning and cultural styles and not to make generalizations about a particular group based upon culture and learning styles. An example would be to conclude that all young African-American males have the same traits as the targeted group.
2. Caution should also be taken in attempting to explain the achievement differences between minority and nonminority students; this is especially true when academic differences are used to explain deficits.
3. One's philosophical beliefs and issues should not influence decisions relevant to the relationship between learning and culture styles.

Hilliard (1989) suggested in his research that the relationship between learning style and culture may prove to be divisive, especially as it relates to students in elementary and secondary schools. It may result in generalizations about culture and style and may lead to discriminating treatment. For example, it may be used as an excuse for student failure. Finally, there is an implication that some styles are more valuable than others even though learning style should be neutral. Properly used, however, matching learning and culture styles can be an effective tool for improving the learning of young African-American males.

THE RELATIONSHIP BETWEEN LEARNING AND INSTRUCTIONAL STYLES

There is some indication that teachers choose instructional styles that closely approximate their own learning preferences. The key to the learning/instructional style theory, however, is that students learn more effectively through their own preference in learning styles (Hilliard, 1989).

Matching instructional and learning styles may also have implications for student achievement. The best way for schools to adapt to individual differences is to increase their effect by differentiated instructional techniques (Guild, 1994). According to Hilliard (1989), a careful match between learning styles and instructional styles may not be the only factor that affects student achievement. For example, the reason younger students do not learn may not be because they cannot learn from instructors using styles that do not match their learning styles, as well as instructors not being flexible enough to change their learning styles and teaching approaches. Additionally, there is not sufficient research or models to relate specific pedagogy to learning styles. Until appropriate instructional models are developed, he recommended that teachers be more sensitive to learning styles in the instructional programs.

IMPLICATIONS FOR EDUCATION

Traditionally, teachers teach and assess students in ways that benefit those with certain learning styles, while placing many other children at a marked disadvantage. Athanases (1993) noted that by keying teaching and assessment to the diverse ways people think and learn, teachers will be surprised at how much smarter their students get.

All individuals favor a preferred style; however, they may vary their styles depending upon the situation. Teachers should be flexible in their teaching and use a variety of styles to ensure that all students' needs are met. Teachers, generally, are best at instructing children whose styles of learning match their own. Consequently, the more students differ from the cultural, socioeconomic, or ethical values of the teacher, the greater the likelihood that their learning needs will not be met. Studies have shown that students receive higher grades and more favorable evaluations when their styles more closely match those of their teachers. Further, most students begin to experience success when they are permitted to pursue an interest in their preferred learning style (Athanases, 1993; Gregorc, 1993).

SUMMARY

The preponderance of research on cultural and learning styles of minority individuals has demonstrated the value of matching these two styles to facilitate the learning process. It is widely believed that such matching can facilitate classroom instruction and provide young African-American males with the skills necessary to succeed in school. Despite some caution in matching cultural, learning, and teaching styles when applied to educating minority individuals, there is little disagreement in the professional literature concerning the relationship between learning and culture styles and their impact on academic and social success in school.

Research conducted over the last decade has revealed certain learning patterns as being characteristic of certain minority groups (Hilliard, 1989; Shade & Edwards, 1989; Vasquez, 1991; Bert & Bert, 1992). African-American groups, for example, tend to use oral experiences, physical activity, and interpersonal relationships over other approaches and patterns. The implications for instructional intervention for these individuals should be self-evident.

As indicated earlier, there is not universal agreement on the application of cultural and learning styles to instruction. Some advocate that applying cultural and learning styles to the instructional process will enable educators to be more sensitive to cultural differences. Others maintain that pinpointing cultural values will lead to stereotyping (Guild, 1994).

Another controversy evolves around the extent to which culture and learning affect achievement. Research findings have consistently pointed to serious inequities when schools do not value or accept certain cultural values. Some studies have shown that incorporating cultural and learning styles in the learning process does not significantly increase achievement unless inequities in delivery/instructional procedures are improved (Hilliard, 1989; Bennet, 1986).

A third controversy centers around how teachers operating from their own cultures and learning styles can successfully teach minority populations. Most of the research shows that caring teachers who provide opportunities for children to learn are more valuable than careful matching of teaching and learning styles (Taylor, 1992; Guild, 1994).

The major issue at hand in this controversy is not whether learning and cultural styles should be incorporated in the instructional plan for young African-American males, but whether information about cultural and learning styles will assist teachers in recognizing diversity and thereby improving delivery of educational services.

4

Practical Application of Social Learning Theories to Educating Young African-American Males

Social learning theories offer the school a common context in which the environment, developmental sequence, and early experiences of young African-American males can be understood and researched. These theories enable the educators to better understand how these children think and how they feel about themselves. They also make educators more aware of factors in the environment that precipitate cognitive and affective problems that may have some bearing on academic performance.

The importance of teaching social skills to African-American males has been well documented. Thus, the preponderance of research strongly supports the notion of teaching and integrating social skills into the curriculum while emphasizing that social skills should assume a position of primacy along with the basic three R's (Hilliard, 1989; Deal, 1990; Bilken, 1990; Forest, 1990; Collins and Hatch, 1992; Kagan, 1989; Johnson & Johnson, 1990).

TYPES OF SOCIAL SKILL DEFICITS

There are four major types of social skills deficits: (1) skill deficits, (2) inadequate skill performance, (3) performance deficits, and (4) self-control deficits.

> 1. Skill deficits occur when individuals do not know how to perform the social skill in question.

2. Inadequate skill performance implies that the individual has partly performed the social skill but, due to lack of understanding, has not completed it. An example may be when somebody is blamed for an act he/she did not commit. Initially, the person would say he/she did not commit the act. However, when the other individual keeps insisting, the accused individual may resort to aggressive behavior rather than using negotiation strategies.

3. Performance deficits indicate that the individual knows how to perform a given task but due to physical or other problems, does not complete it.

4. Self-control deficits include a variety of behaviors in which the individual cannot control his/her behavior. A multitude of problems may be with this deficit. Frequently individuals have to be taught how to control their behaviors. (Specific techniques will be summarized in Chapter 5.)

EFFECTS OF SOCIAL SKILLS DEFICITS

Social skills training should assume an important place in curricula for young African-American males. An increasing number of young African-American males fail to succeed in school because of inadequate social skills. It has been suggested that social skills deficits not only interfere with success in the peer group and educational mainstream, but are also predictive of long-term maladaptive behavior patterns including delinquency, dropping out of school, military discharge for bad conduct, and adult mental health problems.

As a result, acquisition of social communication skills is extremely important for these boys, primarily because social communication skills are the foundation of interpersonal competence. Inclusion of social skills training in curriculum and specific lesson plan design provides the classroom teacher with the opportunity to effectively address social skills deficits.

Research has shown that social skills training packages promote acquisition of socially appropriate behaviors, but there is little evidence to suggest that instruction directed at improving students' social competence transfers over time and across cultural settings. Several reasons for this generalization have been presented.

First, social interaction is reciprocal; it involves social exchange among individuals. The limitations and the absence of socially competent peers as models for young African-American males may seriously impair this reciprocity. Training must take place in settings where these students interact with their peers in order for newly acquired skills to be generalized and maintained.

Second, exposure to adequate peer models is insufficient; peers must be trained to provide appropriate models for young Black males (Holland, 1987). Further, social skills training and reinforcement must occur in settings in which these boys interact naturally with their peers (Taylor, 1994).

Third, young African-American males must be taught to exhibit behaviors that will be reinforced naturally by peers. Therefore, it is important to select target behaviors that are adaptive and desirable, contribute to the development of social competence, and prompt peer responses that are likely to be reinforcing. The lack of social skills training, inappropriate behavioral activity, and poor interpersonal relationship problems all result in deficits in social skills.

Research has shown a positive relationship between certain social skills and school achievement of young African-American males. For example, acts of social communication such as initiating contact about work assignments, asking and answering questions, and engaging in academic-related discussions are experiences needed for appropriate social exchange (Holland, 1987; Hilliard, 1989; Taylor, 1992). Teachers tend to place less value on these social communication skills, however; thus, few opportunities for development of social communication are likely to be provided in classrooms for young African-American males. Systematic assessment procedures are needed to aid the teacher in employing appropriate intervention strategies.

ASSESSING SOCIAL SKILLS

Several tests are available for assessing social skills of young African-American males. These tests measure all aspects of social behavior and may be classified as formal or informal. Since many of these tests were designed for different populations, they will have to be modified for use with young African-American males.

Assessing Social Skills Deficits

Several types of instruments may be used to assess social skills. Commonly used teacher-made tests use several testing formats. These include checklists, observation schedules, rating scales, interviews, direct observations, role play, assessment of social competence, and a variety of inventories covering the gamut of social behaviors. (Examples of assessment inventories appear in Appendices B and C.)

Anecdotal records may also be used in obtaining data about pupils. These records provide an opportunity to study a pupil's behavior over a period of time as well as collecting information that is essential in planning instructional programs. Additionally, anecdotal records provide a means of understanding the dynamics of the learner over a period of time.

McClelland (1992) stressed the importance of assessing children's social skills during the early years using both formal and informal techniques. One of the techniques discussed is the Social Attributes Checklist. Areas covered in the checklist include 8 individual, 14 social skills, and 2 peer relationship attributes. Results from the checklist pinpoint areas of social development in the above attributes that need to be addressed.

The Pediatric Evaluation of Disabilities Inventory is a measure of functional skills in the social function domain. It is also a checklist-type inventory. Haltiwanger (1992) used this checklist with a large sample of parents of young children. A major component of the study was to interview these parents to determine the amount of assistance they provided their children for each skill on the checklist. Analysis of the responses showed that children who were successful received at least minimal assistance or supervision from their parents.

Few tests are designed specifically to assess social skills of young African-American males. As indicated, most tests have to be modified to assess the social traits of this unique group of males. The reader is referred to the latest issue of Buros' Mental Measurements Year Book for additional tests.

Social skills are difficult to assess due chiefly to issues related to reliability, and interpretability. Many social skills are directly associated with one's culture and when assessed outside of that culture, results can be misleading. Assessment instruments for measuring social skills should be interpreted with the uniqueness of the individual in mind and the type of intervention that is being attempted to change the negative behavior.

APPLICATION OF BEHAVIORAL INTERVENTION STRATEGIES

Learning depends upon the following factors: drive, response, cue, and reward. The principal theoretical concepts drawn from this assumption are reinforcement *values* and *expectations*. The tendency for behavior to occur in any given situation is a function of the individual's expectations of reinforcement in that situation and of the value of the reinforcements.

The reinforcement values and expectations of some young African-American males differ from the values expected at school. Thus, what has been successful for them in their environments may be a source of conflict in the school. In essence, these children have frequently been reinforced by what the school may term "negative behaviors." The goal-driven behaviors, responses to events, and the cues they have developed are frequently a means of survival in their environments. These behaviors work well for them until they attend school. At school, the copying and imitative tendencies learned at home are generally not tolerated or accepted, causing frustration, poor self-image, and sometimes aggressive behavior (Villegas, 1991; Bronfenbrenner, 1979).

Most children can learn from rewards and punishments, and then proceed to make a judgment in a new social situation as a result of previous experiences (Gresham & Elliott, 1989). "Social referencing" involves using information from other people to guide behavior and affect ambiguous situations (Obiakor, 1992).

Unfortunately, many at-risk young African-American males cannot learn effective social skills without direct intervention. Frequently, behavior problems arise in class because successful intervention techniques have not been tried. Most traditional methods do not work for many young African-American males. A learning environment is needed that fosters reduction of negative behaviors and recognizes the uniqueness of the individual.

One intervention strategy that appeared to reduce aggressive behavior among males was used by Hudley (1993). A sample (101) of aggressive and nonaggressive elementary-school boys were randomly assigned to an attributional intervention and a nontreatment control group. The study was designed to determine the effects of an attribution intervention program on reducing aggressive males' tendency toward ambiguous negative peer interactions. Findings revealed that the experimental group of boys (attributional intervention) showed a significant reduction in hostile intent and disciplinary action as rated by their teachers (Hudley, 1992, 1993).

Research by Jewett (1992) focused on aggression and cooperation and ways of helping young children use appropriate strategies for coping with them. Jewett asserted that aggression and cooperation share one common element, which emerges from children's strong developmental push to initiate, control, and maintain relationships with their peers.

Aggression was defined as any intentional act that resulted in physical or mental injury. Aggressive actions can be accidental, instrumental, or hostile acts of behavior. It was noted that aggression should not be confused with assertion. Assertion, in turn, was defined as a process or behavior through which children maintain and defend their rights.

Cooperation, on the other hand, was defined as any activity that involves willing interdependence of two or more students. Cooperation was distinguished from compliance in that compliance denoted obedience to authority rather than intentional cooperation. Aggressive behavior may be reduced by employing strategies that permit students to verbalize their feelings, develop appropriate problem-solving techniques to conflict, and internalize and be cognizant of the effects of their aggressive behaviors upon others.

Collins and Hatch (1992) summed up effective strategies for supporting social and emotional growth of young children: (1) model social behavior; (2) establish environments that encourage positive social exchange; (3) encourage children to become aware of the consequences of their behaviors; (4) help children produce acceptable behavior; and (5) encourage the development of children's self-esteem. These behavioral techniques are also designed to make individuals aware of their impact on reacting to and interacting with others.

SUMMARY

One of the valuable roles of teachers is that of being an observer. Observing behavior in the classroom provides valuable information for intervention. Frequently, on the basis of the information supplied, appropriate action can be taken to change negative behaviors. The same rationale may be advanced for other interventions. Equally important is the interpretation of the information from assessment for young African-American males. It is recommended here that resource individuals knowledgeable about Black cultures be consulted before intervention is attempted.

5

Direct Intervention Techniques for Teaching Social Skills

Intervention should reflect the assessed social skills needs of young African-American males. For this purposes, teacher-made checklists may be used as outlined in Chapter 4. Several approaches may be used to promote the pro-social skills of young African-American males.

McGinnis and Goldstein, (1984) supported the concept of direct instruction of social skills, recommending modeling, role playing, practice, and feedback as principal procedures and techniques to teach social skills. Additional instruction using the techniques discussed in this chapter can facilitate the teaching of social skills through direct instruction.

"Direct instruction" implies that the teacher is directly intervening to bring about a desired change. Directed instruction is to be used with any subject area to assist children in learning basic skills, as well as employing the concept of task analysis (step-by-step sequence of learning task).

DIRECT INSTRUCTION FRAMEWORK

Bandura (1977) provided us with the conceptual framework for using direct instruction, advancing the concepts of Social Learning Theory and Behavioral Modeling. He advocated that much of what we learned is through modeling from observing others. Information that is carefully and systematically gained through modeling may be transferred to other academic, social, and nonacademic functions. Specific techniques for using effective modeling strategies will be delineated later in this chapter.

Skillstreaming

Skillstreaming is a comprehensive social skill program developed by McGinnis and Goldsetin (1984).[1] Social skills are clustered in several categories with specific skills to be demonstrated to foster human interaction skills needed to perform appropriate social acts. Clear directions are provided for forming the skillstreaming groups, conducting group meetings, and specifying rules. Activities include modeling, role playing, feedback, and transfer training. Feedback received in the form of praise, encouragement, and constructive criticism is designed to reinforce correct performance of the skills.

Cognitive Behavior Modification

These techniques focus on having individuals think about and internalize their feelings and behaviors before reacting. The process involves learning responses from the environment by listening, observing, and imitating others. Both cognition and language processes are mediated in solving problems and developing patterns of behaviors.

Cognitive behavioral strategies are designed to increase self-control of behavior through self-monitoring, self-evaluation, and self-reinforcement. The strategies assist children in internalizing their behaviors, comparing their behaviors against predetermined standards, and providing positive and negative feedback to themselves. Research findings indicate that there is a positive relationship between what individuals think about themselves and the types of behaviors they display (Rizzo & Zabel, 1988). This premise appears to be true for young African-American males as well. Matching the cognitive and affective process in designing learning experiences for the individuals appears to be realistic and achievable within the school.

Behavior Modification Techniques

Behavioral modification techniques provide the teacher with strategies for assisting children in performing desirable and appropriate behaviors, as well as promoting socially acceptable behaviors. It is a method to modify children's behavior to the extent that when a behavior is emitted in a variety of situations, it becomes consistently more appropriate.

Some cautions have been mentioned for teachers using behavioral strategies in the classroom. The chief purpose of using this technique is to change or modify behaviors. The teacher is not generally concerned with the cause of the behaviors, rather with observing and recording overt behaviors. These behavioral responses may be measured and quantified in any attempt to explain behaviors. There are occasions however, when motivation and the dynamic causes of the behaviors are primary concerns for the teacher.

In spite of the cautions involving using behavioral modification techniques, most of the research supports its use (Salend & Whittaker, 1992; Lane and McWhirter, 1992; Rizzo & Zabel, 1988; Katz, 1991; Taylor, 1992). The major concerns voiced were that the technique must be systematically employed, the environmental constraints must be considered, and teachers, educators, and parents must be well versed in using the technique.

There are many ways in which behavior can be modified. Contingency contracting, the task-centered approach, and peer mediation are three of the most promising techniques:

Contingency Contracting. This technique involves pupils in planning and executing contracts. Gradually, pupils take over record-keeping, analyze their own behavior, and even suggest the timing for cessation of contracts. Micro-contracts are made with the pupil in which he/she agrees to execute some amount of low-probability behavior after which he/she may engage immediately in a high-probability behavior (Pre-mack Principle) for a specified time. An example may be an individual who likes to play sports will be denied the opportunity to play until homework assignments have been completed.

Peer Mediation Strategies. Peer mediation strategies have been successfully employed to manage behavior. The model is student driven and enables students to make decisions about issues and conflicts that have an impact upon their lives. The model requires that students exercise self-regulation strategies, which involves generating socially appropriate behavior in the absence of external control imposed by teachers or other authorities. To be effective, the concept must be practiced and frequently reinforced through role models and demonstrations of pro-social skills.

Several investigations have shown that negative behaviors and discipline problems decrease when this strategy is used. For example, increase in cooperative relationships and academic achievement often follows. Findings also show an increase in task behaviors (Salend & Whittaker, 1992; Lane & McWhirter, 1992). Using this strategy with young African-American males may assist them in internalizing appropriate behaviors.

Task-Centered Approach. The task-centered approach to learning is another way to modify behavior. Pupils may be experiencing difficulty because they cannot grasp certain social skills concepts. Behavioral problems may stem from the frustration of repeated failure, such as poor attention or the inability to work with independently or in groups. This system provides children a highly structured learning environment. Elements in the task-centered approach may include activities to promote:

1. Attention-level tasks designed to gain and hold the pupils' attention.
2. Development of visual and auditory discrimination activities as needed.
3. Interpretation and reaction to social-level tasks emphasizing skills related to social interaction.
4. Imitation of social exchanges, the development of verbal and social courtesies, and group participation activities.

Coaching

Appropriate coaching techniques may be employed by teachers to develop social skills for young African-American males. Some of the commonly known techniques include (1) participation, (2) paying attention, (3) cooperation, (4) taking turns, (5) sharing, (6) communication, and (7) offering assistance and encouragement. These techniques are designed to make individuals cognizant of using alternative methods to solving problems; anticipating the consequences of their behaviors; and developing plans for successfully coping with problems.

Cueing

Cueing is employed to remind students to act appropriately just before the correct action is expected rather after an action is performed incorrectly. This technique is an excellent way of reminding students about prior standards and instruction. A major advantage is that it can be employed anywhere, using a variety of techniques such as glances, hand signals, pointing, nodding or shaking the head, and holding up the hand, to name but a few.

Cueing can be utilizing without interrupting the instructional program or planned activities. The technique assists in reducing negative practices and prevents students from performing inappropriate behaviors.

Successful implementation of this technique requires that students thoroughly understand the requirement, as well as recognize the specific cue. Otherwise, the result may be confused students, especially when they are held accountable for not responding appropriately to the intended cue.

Social-Cognitive Approaches

These techniques are designed to instruct students and to help students maintain better control over their behaviors, deal more effectively with social matters through self-correction and problem solving. Self-monitoring or instruction involves verbal prompting by the student concerning his/her social behavior. Verbal prompting may be overt or covert.

Making Better Choices. This social-cognitive approach is designed to assist students in making better choices. Group lessons are developed around improving social skills. Specifically, lessons promote forethought before engaging in a behavior and to examine the consequences of the behavior. The major components of this program include the following cognitive sequence:

- Stop (inhibit response)
- Plan (behaviors leading to positive behaviors)
- Do (follow plan and monitor behavior)
- Check (evaluate the success of the plan)

These steps are practiced by the students and reinforced by the teacher. Various social skills are identified by the teacher for the student to practice. Progress reports are kept and assessed periodically by both teachers and students.

Modeling

Modeling assumes that an individual will imitate the behaviors displayed by others. The process is considered important because children acquire social skills through replicating behaviors demonstrated by others. Educators and adults may employ modeling techniques to change and influence behaviors by demonstrating appropriate skills to model. The impact and importance of this valuable technique is often overlooked by teachers, who frequently fail to assess the impact of their behaviors on children.

Modeling, if used appropriately, may influence or change behaviors more effectively than demonstration of behavior. This is premised upon the fact that once a behavior pattern is learned through imitation, it is maintained without employing positive reinforcement techniques. Teachers should be apprised and cognizant of the importance of modeling for promoting appropriate social skills. Additionally, they should be trained and exposed to various techniques to facilitate the process.

Children do not automatically imitate models they see. Several factors are involved (1) rapport established between teachers and children; (2) reinforcing consequences for demonstrating or not demonstrating the modeled behavior; and (3) determining the appropriate setting for modeling certain behaviors (Bandura, 1963).

Students should be taught how to show or demonstrate positive behaviors by observing others performing positive behaviors in structured situations. The technique provides for the structured learning of appropriate behaviors through examples and demonstration by others. Internal or incidental modeling may occur at any time and modeling activities may be infused throughout the curriculum at random. However, a regular structured time or period of day is recommended in order to develop structure in a variety of social conditions. Teaching behavioral skills through modeling is best accomplished by beginning with impersonal situations that most students encounter, such as the correct way to show respect for others. Activities should be planned based upon the assessed needs of the class and be flexible enough to allow for changes when situations dictate. As students master the modeling process, additional behavioral problems may be emphasized.

Role Playing

Role playing is an excellent technique for allowing children to act out both appropriate and inappropriate behaviors without embarrassment, or experiencing the consequences of their actions. It permits students to experience hypothetical conditions that may cause anxiety or emotional responses in ways that may enable them to better understand themselves. Once entrenched, these activities may be transferred to real-life experiences.

Role playing may assist students in learning appropriate social skills through developing appropriate models by observing and discussing alternative behavioral approaches. Role playing may be conducted in any type of classroom structure, level, or group size. It may be individually or group induced. Through appropriate observations and assessment procedures, areas of intervention may be identified for role-playing activities.

Role playing assists children in identifying and solving problems within a group context. It is also beneficial to shy students. It encourages their interactions with classmates without aversive consequences. As with most group activities, role playing must be structured. Activities should be designed to reduce, minimize, correct, or eliminate identified areas of deficits through the assessment process.

Gill (1991) listed the following advantages of role playing:

· Allows the student to express hidden feelings.
· Is student-centered and addresses the needs and concerns of the student.
· Permits the group to control the content and pace.
· Enables the student to empathize with others and understand their problems.
· Portrays generalized social problems and dynamics of group interaction, formal and informal.
· Gives more reality and immediacy to academic descriptive material (History, Geography, Social Skills, English).
· Enables the student to discuss private issues and problems.
· Provides an opportunity for nonarticulate students and emphasizes the importance of nonverbal and emotional responses.
· Gives practice in various types of behavior.

Disadvantages include:

· The teacher can lose control over what is learned and the order in which it is learned.
· Simplifications can mislead.
· It may dominate the learning experiences to the exclusion of solid theory and facts.
· It is dependent upon the personality, quality, and mix of the teacher and students.
· It may be seen as too entertaining and frivolous.

Gill (1991) investigated the effects of role play, modeling, and videotape playback on the self-concept of elementary-school children, 13% of whom were African-Americans. The Piers-Harris Children's Self-Concept Scale was employed on a pre/posttest basis. Intervention was for a six-month period. Data showed that the combination of role playing, modeling, and videotape playback had some effect upon various dimensions of self-concept.

Videotape Modeling

Videotape modeling is an effective way to improve self-concept. Children may be encouraged to analyze classroom behavior and patterns of interaction through reviewing videotapes. In this way, children can see the behaviors expected before they are exposed to them in various settings. Videotape modeling affords teachers the opportunity to reproduce the natural conditions of any behavior in the classroom setting. Consequently, videotape modeling may provide realistic training that can be transferred to real experiences inside and outside of the classroom.

For young African-American males, educators may employ this technique to help transfer modeling skills to real-life situations. It has been proven as an effective tool to teach pro-social skills to this group.

COOPERATIVE LEARNING

A basic definition of cooperative learning is "learning through the use of groups." Five basic elements of cooperative learning are:

- · Positive interdependence
- · Individual accountability
- · Group processing
- · Small group/social skills
- · Face-to-face primitive interaction

A cooperative group is one in which two or more students work together toward a common goal in which every member of the group is included. Learning together in small groups has proven to provide a sense of responsibility and an understanding of the importance of cooperation among youngsters (Adams, 1990; Schultz, 1990). Children need to socialize and interact with each other. Among the best known cooperative structures are Jigsaw, Student Teams Achievement Divisions (STAD), Think-Pair-Share, Group Investigation, Circle of Learning, and Simple Structures.

Cooperative learning strategies have the power to transform classrooms by encouraging communities of caring, supportive students whose achievements improve and whose social skills grow (Kagan, 1990). Harnessing and directing the power of cooperative learning strategies present a challenge to the classroom teacher, however. Decisions about the content appropriateness of the structures, the necessary management routings, and the current social skill development of the learners call for special teacher preparation (Johnson, Johnson, & Holubec, 1988; Allen, 1990). For successful outcomes with students, teachers also need the follow-up of peer coaches, administrative support, parent understanding, and time to adapt to the strategies (Slavin, 1991).

While cooperative models replace individual seat work, they continue to require individual accountability. Thus, teachers who use cooperative learning structures recognize that it is important for students to both cooperate and compete.

To use a cooperative structure effectively, teachers need to make some preliminary decisions. According to Kagan (1989), the following questions should be asked:

· What kind of cognitive and academic development does it foster?
· What kind of social development does it foster?
· Where in the lesson plan (content) does it best fit?

Teachers also need to examine what conditions increase the effect of cooperative strategies. Positive interdependence, face-to-face (primitive) interaction, individual accountability, and group processing affect cooperative learning outcomes.

The benefits of cooperative learning appear to be reflected in the following:

· Academic gains, especially among minority and low-achieving students.
· Improved race relations among students in integrated classrooms.
· Improved social and affective development among students (Kagan, 1989; Johnson et al., 1988; Slavin, 1991).

Cooperative learning practices vary tremendously. The models can be complex or simple. Whatever their design, cooperative strategies include:

· A common goal
· A structured task
· A structured team
· Clear roles
· Designated time frame
· Individual accountability
· A structured process

We need cooperative structures in our classrooms because many traditional socialization practices are absent. Not all students come to school with a social orientation, and students appear to master content more efficiently with these structures (Kagan, 1989). The preponderance of research indicates that cooperative learning strategies motivate students to care about each other and to share responsibility in completing tasks. (Refer to Appendix D for some Cooperative Learning Strategies to use in the classroom.)

Cooperative Learning vs. Peer Tutoring

It is frequently assumed by parents that cooperative learning is another aspect of peer tutoring, but there are many significant differences between cooperative learning and peer tutoring. In cooperative learning, everyone is responsible for learning and nobody is acting as a teacher or a tutor.

On the other hand, in peer tutoring, one child plays the role of the teacher and another that of student or tutor. Thus, the initial teaching does not come from a student, but from a teacher because all students are exposed to basic concepts in a group. The tutor already knows the subject and material and teaches it to a peer who needs individualized remedial help to master a specific skill. Those who grasp concepts quickly become the designated tutor. These students reinforce what they have just learned by explaining concepts and skills to teammates who need help (Slavin, 1991).

Cooperative work puts a heterogeneous group of students together to share ideas and knowledge.

SPECIAL GROUP ACTIVITIES

In a paper presented at the annual meeting of the American Education Research Association, Dorr-Bremme (1992) advanced some unique techniques for improving social identity in kindergarten and first grade. Students sat in groups and planned daily activities; these activities were videotaped. Analysis of the videotapes revealed several dimensions of social identity to be important, such as academic capability, maturity, talkativeness, independence, aggressiveness, ability to follow through, and leadership ability. The teacher responded to students individually and as circle participants, depending upon how the behavior was viewed.

Findings indicated that social identity was the combined responsibility of everyone in the classroom interacting to bring about the most positive social behavior. Interactions between individual students and the teacher were minimized.

BLACK MALE VOLUNTEERS' PROGRAM

In an effort to improve education among African-American males, some authorities advocate an increase in the presence of African-American male role models. This approach is designed to prevent the development of negative attitudes toward the school environment and promote high levels of academic achievement. It is felt that the African-American male teacher in the early grades can have a remarkable effect on the students, especially in the inner city where single-parent, female-headed households are commonplace. It is important that African-American males have the opportunity to be a part of an environment where an African-American male role model shows concern for young Black males. When this occurs, the African-American male child's self-esteem and academic achievement most likely will improve. Project 2000 and The Educational Opportunity Program have demonstrated the importance of involving Black male role models in educating young African-American males.

Project 2000

Project 2000 is a program implemented by The Center for Educating African-American Males at Morgan State University for three Baltimore City Elementary Schools. Project 2000 is modeled after a successful role model program implemented in 1988 at Stanton Elementary School in Southeast Washington, D.C.

Using a network of business, community, and civic leaders, the center recruited adult males, particularly African-Americans, to serve as teacher assistants for one-half day per week in the classrooms of kindergarten through third grade students. The major objective was to prevent the development of negative attitudes toward the school environment and to promote high levels of academic achievement among African-American males in the early grades by providing them with adult role models in their daily school experience.

The Educational Opportunity Program (E.O.P.)

The position that Black males would do better if they were exposed to positive Black male role models was experimented with through this project, which was designed to assign selected males to serve as tutors to young Black males. Initial results show that the project is having a significant impact on reducing aggressive and negative behaviors and on increasing achievement, attendances, and positive attitudes toward girls and female authorities (Gibbs, 1991).

Male volunteers were carefully screened and recruited from a variety of businesses and organizations in both the public and private sectors. Volunteers came from all occupational levels and pledged to spend one-half day per visit with the boys. Visits were planned in advance in order that the classroom teacher would have time to augment the instructional program. Volunteers performed many duties and tasks such as accompanying the class on field trips, assisting with discipline problems, checking seatwork and homework, monitoring laboratories, tutoring in academic subjects, duplicating materials, and designing games and activities to promote social growth.

Holland's (1992) view of using Black male models support the aforementioned position. According to Holland, if Black men do not return to the schools to assist in educating Black males and identifying with them, we will lose them to a world of crime and dope. Additionally, he stated that Black male models exercise more control over young Black males because young Black males want their attention and approval.

The reader should exercise caution in using this strategy, and legal advice is recommended, as the strategy has been challenged as a violation of civil rights. As a compromise, some school districts are using male and female volunteers with both girls and boys in integrated classes.

The E.O.P. Program, facilitated by Nathaniel McFadden at Lake Clifton-Eastern Senior High School in Baltimore, Maryland was designed to improve the social and academic skills of African-American male students. The program's objectives were to keep students from dropping out of school and to inspire them to go to college (The Abell Report, 1991).

Programs such as these have proven effective in the African-American community. In the first group trained from 1986 to 1990, 51 participants graduated from high school; 6 more completed high school within the year 1991; 49 were admitted to college (The Abell Report, 1991).

Positive effects have been obtained in the Project 2000 Program as well. In an all-male first-grade class in Baltimore City, school officials stated that they have seen dramatic improvements. Only 1 of the 20 students involved in the program was below grade level. Discipline problems almost disappeared and attendance improved significantly. These two programs have shown that young African-American males can significantly benefit from the guidance of

African-American male role models (Brown, 1991; Stewart & England, 1989).

Young African-American males are in desperate need for African-American role models, especially male. According to Wright (1992), a significant percentage of Black boys are from single-parent homes, usually headed by a female. As a result, the child's early childhood is frequently dominated by females. Wright (1992) affirmed that these young boys need legitimate Black male role models in their lives.

Mancus (1992) postulated that the absence of positive male role models in impoverished urban neighborhoods and the feminization of the African-American family are given as the primary justification for assigning Black male teachers to classes of African-American male students. Studies have indicated that primary students' perceptions of a school, teachers, and programs are influenced by teacher gender (Sloan, 1992). It is predicted, therefore, that boys will be more likely to see themselves as academically competent, thus, more inclined to achievement, when they have Black male teachers. Also, they will be more likely to share authority and express nurturing behavior when they see male teachers doing so. This premise further supports the need for African-American males as teachers and role models.

Effects of Fatherless Households

Gaeddert (1992) noted that it is from other people's actions that we become familiar with society's demands and the rules we are expected to obey as we imitate or selectively respond to models during social learning. According to Gaeddert (1992), males and females generally choose same-sex models. Therefore, the absence of fathers is likely to have adverse effects on the young African-American male child. A Black child born today has only a one in five chance of growing up with two parents until the age of 16 (Ingrassia, 1993). Two out of three births to Black women under 35 are out of wedlock (Smith, 1993). In the inner city, at least 40% of Black children are raised in fatherless homes (Shades & Edwards, 1987).

In these fatherless homes, a child is more likely to live in poverty. The 1990 census figures show that 65% of the children of Black single mothers were poor (Ingrassia, 1993). As such, they are exposed to greater risks, educationally and socially. Additionally, they are not likely to be promoted with their peers and probably will drop out of school sooner (Ingrassia, 1993). Mothers can be smothering, especially if her son is the only man in her life (Smith, 1993). Ingrassia (1993) noted that the boys in particular need male role models. Without a father, who will help them define what it means to be a man? Fathers do things for their children that mothers often do not. Though there are obviously exceptions, fathers typically encourage independence and a sense of adventure, while mothers tend to be more nurturing and protective. It is men that teach boys how to be fathers.

Because of a lack of readily accessible models to positively influence young African-American males' development, North Carolina has developed a Black male role model program (1987) designed to provide male influence in the lives of young African-American males. Data from the project indicate that the project has had a significant impact upon the behaviors of Black males.

Without a father, young Black males learn many negative attitudes which may have adverse affects upon their lives. This often means gangs, from which the message is that "women are whores and handmaidens, not equals" (Ingrassia 1993: 17-29). This kind of mentality has led to separation of the sexes among African Americans. Having a male role model that can enlighten the young child's understanding may help deter this way of thinking. The presence of the African-American male can serve this purpose, as many children otherwise would not have the presence of a father figure that can provide the guidance and caring so many young African-American males need.

Lapoint (1992) concluded that African-American male adults must become new role models of empowerment and advocacy to our youth, for if we do not teach and show them that we care about the quality of their lives, how else will they learn how to care and take responsibility for themselves?

In the absence of a father or a Black role model, many young African-American males are influenced by their environments. They may succumb to environments that are filled with vices and illegal influences. These types of environments foster the following statistics:

· One out of every 22 at-risk Black American males will be killed by violent crime.
· Fifty-one percent of violent crimes in the United States is committed by at-risk Black youths.
· One out of every six at-risk Black males will be arrested by the time they reach 19.
· Eighty-six percent of at-risk Black youth live in poverty (Ingrassia, 1993; Lapoint, 1992).
· One out of 3 young Black males are somewhere in the Justice System (Thomas, 1995).

Black Teachers As Role Models

African American Male teachers are few in number. Ironically, this is in contrast to the increasing Black student enrollment in urban elementary and secondary schools (Wiley, 1991; Graham, 1987). Recent data show that with the dwindling minority teacher representation, it is possible that a minority student could complete the K-12 school experience without ever meeting a minority teacher (Rancifer, 1991). This is unfortunate for the African-American students, as they are in a desperate need of African-American role models. As mentioned, many Black students may have low aspirations for school work because they cannot see themselves in a tangible manner in the worthy professions, which includes teaching (Rancifer, 1991).

Moreover, as the proportion of white teachers grows, role models that might encourage minority students to pursue careers in education decreases (Irvine, 1989). Without sufficient exposure to minority teachers throughout their education, both minority and majority students come to characterize the teaching profession, and the academic enterprise in general, as best suited for whites. The presence of the African American role model is needed to address this mentality. In all too many instances, Black peers serve to lower academic achievement by labeling those who do well in school as "wanting to be white," and making it clear that Black boys can either be popular or smart but not both (Gill, 1991).

The continued presence of Black teachers and administrators in the schools, the maintenance of a climate supportive of ethnic pluralism, and the concept of multicultural education, all correlate with maximizing the opportunities for educational excellence for young African-American males. These professional adults are the "significant others" for young African-American males who act as appropriate role models and are capable of enhancing the boys' self-concept. They are particularly important in the lives of children who may otherwise lack daily contact with educated, intelligent, successful Black role models (Lapoint, 1992).

The presence of an African-American male teacher is especially important for these boys, as many of them are from single-parent, female-headed households. Their most significant role models from birth to age four or five have been female relatives (Holland, 1991). Also, the absence of a sturdy and contributing male parent in a major percentage of Black families denies the young African-American male a readily accessible model to positively influence his development (Wake County Public Schools, 1987).

McRae (1994) designed a study to determine if the perceptions of Black and white teachers supported the concept that Black American male teachers made a difference in establishing proper role models for Black boys, as well as positively impacting their self-concepts, social behavior, and academic performance. Thirty-nine educators were interviewed concerning their perceptions toward Black teachers as role models. Two research questions were formulated to guide the research:

· Will African-American male teachers have a significant impact upon the self-concept of African-American male boys?
· Does the presence of African-American male teachers in the classroom have a positive effect upon the academic achievement of African-American boys?

Sample. The sample was randomly selected from Baltimore City elementary teachers attending a local college and educators at an elementary school in the city. Prior permission had been given from the public schools to interview the participants. A total of 39 educators participated in the research project.

Instrument. An interview schedule was constructed and submitted to a panel of experts for validation. Based upon their input, the instrument was modified. The final revised instrument was used to interview participants.

Analysis of Data. All 30 participants completed the interview, yielding a 100% response rate. Of these participants, 30 (77%) were African American: 8 males (21%) and 22 females (56%); white: 3 males (7.6%) and 5 females (12.8%); and 1 (2.6%) Pacific Islander. Years of experience were reported as : (a) 0-2 years, 7 (18%); 3-5 years, 7 (18%); 6-10 years, 8 (21%); 11-15 years, 2 (5%); 16-20 years, 7 (18%); 21-25 years, 4 (10%); 26 or more years, 4 (10%).

The titles of the educators varied. There were 16 (41%) "regular" teachers, 15 (38%) special educators, and one each (2.6%) master teacher, principal, social worker, speech pathologist, resource teacher, assistant principal and counselor.

Data from participants appeared to support the major research questions of this investigation.

Research Question #1:
1. Will African-American male teachers have a significant impact upon the self-concept of African-American male students?

Seventy-two percent (72%) of the participants reported that they believed that their presence would significantly increase the boys' self-esteem. They further articulated that they believed that the boys would see them as caring professionals who could relate to them and encourage them to succeed as well as improve their socialization skills.

Research Question #2:
2. Does the presence of African-American male teachers in the classroom have a positive effect upon the academic achievement of African-American male students?

Participants were in agreement with the research question. A significant percentage (64%) responded that African-American male students being taught by an African-American male teacher would show improvement in achievement. Additionally, they noted that by having an African-American male as a teacher would provide the African-American student with opportunity to see himself as an intelligent, contributing professional, with purpose and promise.

Discussion. Results of this study are in agreement with the majority of research in the field, that is, Black male teachers have a significant impact upon the self-concept and academic achievement of African-American males. Additionally, more African-American male teachers are needed to improve their academic and social skills.

Participants in this study also agreed with the preponderance of research on Black role models which indicates that the presence of an African-American male teacher is especially important for young inner-city boys, many of whom are from single-parent, female-headed households. Their most significant role models from birth to age four or five have been females. The absence of a sturdy and contributing male parent in a major percentage of Black families denies the young African-American male a readily accessible model to positively influence his development.

Many of the special group activities reviewed appear to have significantly impacted upon the social and academic development for young African-American males. The Black male role model program has many merits for educating Black males; however, the legal and civil rights dimensions must be fully explored before attempting such a program.

THE ROLE OF THE SCHOOL IN A BEHAVIOR SETTING

A meaningful approach to dealing with negative behavior would be to isolate the behavior and then quantify, record, and observe the number of acts involved. When this determination has been made, the teacher is equipped to undertake a course of action to change the negative behavior. Social skills training is the technique advocated. Analysis of behavior, using the checklist included in Appendix C, may lead the teacher to pursue a course of action.

All children, including young African-American males, enter school with a wide range of learning abilities, interests, motivation, personalities, attitudes, cultural orientations, and social-economic status. These traits and abilities must be recognized and incorporated into the instructional program (Bankee & Obiakor, 1992).

Pupils also enter school with set behavioral styles. Frequently, these styles are inappropriate for the school. Several techniques are recommended to change inappropriate behaviors in the classroom:

1. Raise the tolerance of the teacher. Teachers generally expect pupils to perform up to acceptable standards. Additionally, they often assume that pupils have been taught appropriate social skills at home. Whereas this may be true for most pupils, frequently it is not true for young African-American males. By recognizing causal factors, such as environment, culture, and values, the teacher's tolerance levels may be raised.

2. Change teacher expectations for pupils. Pupils generally live up to teacher's expectations. Teachers should expect positive behaviors from children. To accomplish this goal, behaviors will sometimes have to be modeled. It is also reocmmended that individual time be allowed for certain pupils through interviews and individual conferences where the teacher honestly relates how the child's behavior is objectional.

3. Analyze teachers' behavior toward a pupil. Pupils use the teacher's overt behavior as a mirror of their strength in the classroom. When a positive reflection is projected, the achievement level is increased. When the message is overtly or covertly negative, the pupil has nothing to support his/her efforts. For example, if there is little positive interaction between pupil and the teacher, the pupil may conclude that his/her behavior is not approved by the teacher. Because the pupil depends so heavily on the teacher's behavior for clues, it is crucial that the teacher objectively analyze his/her interaction with the pupils.

SUMMARY

Most learning is social and is mediated by other people. Consequently, young African-American males, as well as all children, profit when working in groups. Individual and group activities have proven to be successful in teaching appropriate social skills. Behavioral intervention techniques have proven to be equally successful.

Many individual and group experiences have been designed to promote social growth among and between children. One of the most promising of these is cooperative learning. Cooperative learning promotes:

- Positive interdependence
- Face-to-face interaction
- Individual accountability
- Interpersonal and small groups skills
- Group processing (Johnson & John
  son, 1990; Slavin & Oickle, 1981).

Most young African-American males do not attain academic success due partly to their inability to implement the proper social skills. These suggested techniques are designed to reduce student isolation and increase students' abilities appropriately to react and to work with other students toward the solution of common problems. Teachers should experiment with various forms of individual, group, and behavioral intervention strategies to improve the social skills of young African-American males (Taylor, 1992). Since most behaviors are learned, they can be changed through behavioral intervention. Once new social skills are learned through the application of these techniques, they become automatic (refer to Chapter 4 for additional strategies).

Lutfiyya (1991) outlined three strategies for successful group facilitation: (1) facilitation, (2) interpretation, and (3) accommodation. All three approaches depend upon cooperation within the group and roles are shared by all involved. Although this approach is primarily used to diagnose and evaluate disabled individuals, implications for group planning are clear.

Social skills interventions are needed if young African-American males are to be successfully integrated into the mainstream. Activities such as greeting, sharing, cooperating, assisting, complimenting, and inviting should be developed and modeled and infused throughout the curriculum (Anita & Kreimeyer, 1992).

Although the population of African-American children entering school is increasing, the available pool of African-American teachers is declining. This is unfortunate, as the literature has shown that African-American students are in desperate need of African-American role models, especially male.

The African-American child needs to see African-American males with whom they can identify and try to emulate by seeing their employment as worthy professions. They need to see African-American males as intelligent, capable, worthy, and contributing citizens. One of the best ways for this to occur is to have African-American male teachers in the classroom. African-American male teachers may be the only father figure for many urban African-American students since many come from single-parent, female-headed households. In many of these female-headed households, there are no male figures for the young child to positively identify with, such as uncles, grandfathers, or cousins.

The absence of fathers has been identified as contributing to the adverse conditions and, subsequently, the plight of the African-American male today. In the fatherless home, a child is more likely to live in poverty and is a greater risk educationally. Finally, the child is less likely to learn what it means to make and keep a commitment.

Without a male role model in these fatherless homes, the child may be influenced by the environment—environment that is often filled with gangs and individuals dealing in illegal activities. Without African-American male teachers and other positive Black role models, the boys may emulate the inappropriate models to which they have been exposed.

The presence of African-American male teachers, as well as other positive adult African-American male role models, has been proven to be successful. The Project 2000 Program directed by Spencer Holland has already reported success. Similarly, the Educational Opportunity Program (E.O.P.) at the Lake Clifton-Eastern Senior High School in Baltimore, Maryland has also reported success by having African-American male teachers help combat the ills of African-American students' experience.

From these examples, it is evident that the presence of an African-American male teacher as a role model can be instrumental in improving the self-concept and academic achievement of the African-American male child.

NOTE

1. Specific directions for conducting a skillstreaming program may be found in Goldstein, A., & McGinnis, E. (1984) *Skillstreaming the elementary child*. Champagne, IL: Research Press Company.

6

Parental Roles in Social Skills Development

Educators must experiment with innovative ways of involving parents in the school (Harry & McLaughlin, 1992). Over the last several decades, the school has had a difficult time in establishing effective partnerships with parents. Generally, teachers tend to have little interaction with parents. Involvement and interaction may be improved through reporting to parents, holding conferences at times that are conducive for parents to attend, seeking parental assistance in planning and participating in field trips, in serving as resource individuals, tutoring children, and assisting with small groups planning special events.

Much of the noninvolvement has occurred because of hostility or parental indifference toward the school. Many schools serving young African-American males consider their parents a nuisance, unproductive, uneducated, lacking social grace, and not well informed on education and social issues. The relationship is further strained when parents internalize the negative behaviors displayed by the school and come to view the school as a place where they are unaccepted and which has no interest in them as individuals. There must be a total shift in the paradigm. The school must accept these parents and provide training and assistance in desired areas to effectively involve them in the educational process. Parental involvement should become a prime goal for all schools.

Parents may stimulate the social growth and development of their children in various ways. Designing everyday situations for them to explore, providing activities to promote self-esteem and confidence, praising them frequently, providing support, and assisting in creating a healthy and safe environment are but a few positive activities needed for normal child development.

Social changes are constantly occurring in early childhood. During this rapid expanding period, children gain self-awareness and learn how to respond appropriately in different situations. Making sure that appropriate social models are provided is a responsibility of parents. Children who are products of stimulating and positive environments bring a sense of social maturity and independence to the learning environment.   Research findings by Lareau (1987) and Delgado-Gaitan (1991) support the above premise.

Strong families give children an edge in school.   Children who participate in family functions tend to perform better in school than those who did not.   Strong family ties appear to improve children's self-image and confidence. The family is the cornerstone for success in later life.   Parent education appears to play a role in how well students perform in school.

Minority students as a group tend to score lower than white and Asian students in most achievement areas.   Results showed that 38% of Hispanic students obtained high scores while only 16% of Black students obtained high scores.   By comparison, 58% of white and Asian students earned higher scores.

Quality of family life appears to be another significant factor in all groups.   Black students from intact families performed better than those who lived only with their mothers. For example, strong family ties appear to reduce some of the anxiety faced by disadvantaged children. Further, Black children from families who attended church also scored higher on tests (Hilliard, 1988; Lynch, 1987).

Creative and innovative ways to gain family involvement must be experimented with, especially for parents of young African-American males (Mansbach, 1993). Factors such as (1) diverse school experiences, (2) diverse economic and time constraints, and (3) diverse linguistic and cultural practices, all combine to inhibit parental involvements.

Diversity should be recognized as a strength, rather than a weakness. Parents need to feel that their cultural styles and language represent valued knowledge, and that this knowledge is needed and welcomed in the school. One recommended approach is to dialogue with parents in order to understand what they think can be done to improve involvement (Finders & Lewis, 1994).

Unless these strategies are adhered to, children academic and social development will be impeded. The cooperation of school and home is needed if social skills training is to be effective. There is an urgent need to involve parents by making them aware of their important role as well as training them in the home.[1] Several guidelines have been developed for this purpose.

Parental Guidelines for Promoting Social Growth

Young African-American males, as well as other children, follow general developmental milestones in social skills. This predictable sequence permits parents to work with their children where they are developmentally and to pattern the learning of social skills in a more structured manner. Several guidelines are offered to aid parents:

Guideline I. Initially, all learning comes through the five senses. Early experiences should be provided with as many concrete examples as possible using the five senses. Children's self-awareness, discovery, and interests in their environments are enhanced.

Guideline II. Children should be permitted and encouraged to use the "discovery process" as much as possible by experimenting with appropriate social behaviors. Children explore their social world by trying out new behaviors. The effects that these behaviors have on others—how you respond—help shape the direction children will take. Children usually increase social behaviors that are rewarded by positive attention.

Guideline III. Behaviors are learned by imitating others in the environment. The child observes the actions of others and imitates those actions, thus acquiring new skills. Repeating those actions eventually leads to using them in functional situations. As the child develops, he/she is usually eager to imitate the "big kid" ways of older brothers and sisters or other children. This is especially true when applied to parents and other adults.

Guideline IV. Play provides an opportunity for children to learn many social skills. The chief "business" of childhood is play. Children gradually learn the give and take of group play. Enjoying playing near other children comes before the ability to play cooperatively with others. As play skills progress, the child can practice many social roles and act out many social situations within the security of make-believe play.

Guideline V. Having friends is an important part of childhood development. Many social skills are learned such as sharing, taking turns, being a leader and follower, and respecting the rights of others. As children develop, they need the companionship of other people. Follow the child's preference in selecting friends and provide opportunities for frequent play experiences at home and in the neighborhood. As children develop, being accepted and liked by other children becomes increasingly important. Learning to survive squabbles, hurt feelings, and changing affections is part of the normal but sometimes painful process of making friends.

Guideline VI. Praise your child frequently for successful completion of tasks. Provide social activities that ensure success. Set up the social situation for the child to be successful and show your pleasure through hugs, smiles, and perhaps special treats. Step in to help if your child is frustrated and on the brink of failure. Reward the child with plenty of praise for accomplishing what he/she was able to do and having the courage to attempt the rest.

Guideline VII. Provide activities to promote social decision making. Support the child in his decision making. Demonstrate alternate ways of arriving at appropriate decisions. As your child begins to signal definite opinions about his/her world, you can help practice making appropriate decisions. Whenever possible, offer two acceptable choices and let your child make the decision; for example, "Do you want to play inside or outside today?" "Do you want to wear your baseball shirt or your PTA shirt to school?" or "How should you have this done another way?"

Guideline VIII. Teach your child to respect ownership by recognizing others' possessions and property. Gaining a sense of "mine" marks a developmental step in self-awareness. As your Child shows a preference for certain objects, make sure that he/she has ready access to these favorites, if appropriate. Talk about things and people in terms of what belongs to the child and what belongs to others (e.g., his/her shoes, his/her brother/s shoes). Your child may also appreciate a special place within the home to use as a quiet play area and a secure space for treasured possessions.

Guideline IX. Demonstrate appropriate social behaviors in a variety of situations and have children to copy and model appropriate behaviors. Knowing "how to act" in different social situations is not easy for young children. By giving your child clear guidelines for good behavior, rewarding efforts, and giving opportunities to practice, the child will learn patterns of acceptable social skills. For example, practicing a quiet voice or whisper in make-believe play prepares your child for appropriate quiet manners in the library. Acting out the giving of presents can be a rehearsal for a first away-from-home birthday party. Model and teach good manners. Your child will learn from a wide variety of ordinary social experiences, such as going shopping, eating at restaurants, playing in the parks, and visiting friends and relatives. Do not expect your child's social behavior to be perfect. All children lapse into less mature behavior, especially when they are tired, frustrated, or in unfamiliar situations. Do not let the occasional embarrassment of a loud temper tantrum in a crowded shopping mall discourage you. Try to evaluate your child's behavior objectively, noting the successes as well as the problems.

Guideline X. Employ a variety of community resources to promote social experiences through direct participation by the child. Participating in community activities is one way your child can have fun while gaining social experiences with peers. Many communities offer a variety of activities designed to build social skills as:

· Preschool story hour at the library
· Water play and swimming lessons
· Children's films
· Holiday parades
· Holiday parties
· Supervised play at "tot lots"
· Dance classes
· Children's exhibits at museums
· Special events at shopping malls
· Community outreach center
· Community fairs at neighborhood schools

The following are strategies for facilitating the social learning process of young African-American males, as well as all children.

Relate Tasks to the Developmental Level. Some children are eager to start new tasks and experiences. Others need to be coaxed and encouraged. Regardless of how your child approaches challenges, success is important for the development of self-concept. Direct your child toward challenges that he/she is developmentally ready for. Break down big tasks into smaller parts; for example, if your child wants to make a garden, break down the project into small but easy steps—digging, making holes, dropping seeds, covering them, and watering. Show him each step, but let your child do it for himself. Give praise abundantly; avoid criticism whenever possible.

Build a Sense of Security and Trust. Given a loving and responsive home environment, your child will be able to establish a sense of self apart from the people and things about her. Patience, consistency, and loving discipline are acts of caring that support your child as she strives toward independence. Praise the child for tasks well done.

Be Sensitive to Your Child's Signals. As an individual, your child shows unique ways of responding to new people and new experiences. Although he may not be able to put his feelings into words, he may need reassurance when entering into unknown territory. Sometimes fearfulness and negative behaviors are signs that your child is not quite ready for the challenge at hand.

Make Your Child an Equal in the Family. Membership in a family involves learning to share: sharing time, sharing material resources, sharing one another's love. As your child grows more capable, he/she should be given the opportunity to perform tasks that contribute to the functioning of the family. Your child also needs to be shown ways to express how much he cares about the people he loves.

Provide a Good Role Model for Your Child to Emulate. Practice makes perfect. Demonstrate appropriate role models for your child to follow. Children quickly remember what they see.

Be Aware of Your Child's Limitations. Realize that your child's present social capabilities are largely determined by his/her overall developmental level. Your expectations of social behavior should be based on developmental age, not chronological age. Set appropriate and realistic goals based upon the development pattern of your child.

Go From the Known to the Unknown. Prepare your child for new experiences by linking the familiar to the unknown. If your child has met the librarian and visited the children's room in the neighborhood library many times, then participating in preschool story hour is not so scary a prospect.

SUMMARY

From the very beginning, your child has an important place within your family. By being responsive to your child's needs for comfort, play, and love, you build a foundation for positive interactive social relationships. The drive for independence emerges as developmental skills grow. As your child tries to do more and more for himself, he continues to depend on you for guidance and support. Parent delight in the small accomplishments of a child can set expectations for larger successes.

Parents of young African-American males, as well as all parents, have a tremendous influence and impact through appropriate models for developing social skills. The developmental level of the child as well as the developmental sequence must be considered in social skills training.

In order for parents of young African-American males to be effective change agents in promoting appropriate social skills development, early intervention in healthcare, counseling, housing, nutrition, education, and child rearing practices, etc., must be improved. Early intervention and parental involvements are essential for preparing children to master social skill tasks successfully.

When necessary, the school should assume the responsibility of teaching parents how to provide their children with enriched experiences that will provide the necessary foundation for success in school. This approach minimizes failure and promotes positive self-concepts in young African-American males, as well as all children. At-risk young African-American males may lack the necessary experience to be successful in school. Parental training will assist in closing the learning gap.

There has been strong support from the federal government to include the family in the early educational process of their children. For example, the federal government has created guidelines for the educational community to use in developing and implementing a comprehensive, coordinated, multidisciplinary, interagency program of early intervention services for infants, toddlers, and their families (Gallager, 1989).

According to much of the research in the field, the role of parental participation in educating young African-American males has been limited. This view has been interpreted to imply that parents had no interest in the education of their children (Lynch & Stein, 1987; Marion, 1981). Several factors may contribute to the lack of parental participation and involvement. Many parents do not feel welcome in the schools, believing that they have little to offer in educating their children. Further, Cassidy (1988) reported that problems with scheduling, transportation, and knowledge of the instructional programs are partly responsible for poor parental participation.

Parents must feel that they are welcome in the school and be given responsibilities concerned with planning, collaborating with teachers, and policy-making. Parents should have an active role in planning and instructing their children and function as advocates for them if children are to profit significantly from their school experiences.

All persons benefit when an effective working relationship and rapport have been established. Parents should be informed on a regular basis of their children's progress in school. Schools should experiment with various ways of improving parental participation, since they are the foremost educators of their children.

NOTE

1. An excellent book to review for involving African-American mothers in the schools is: Winters, G. (1993). *African American mothers and urban schools*. New York: Lexington Books.

7

Overview: Evaluating Social Skills of Young African-American Males

The relationship between social learning theories and the learning and academic performance of young African-American males is not well established. Most research reported today involves intervention for Black adolescents and youth males. It is necessary, therefore, to conduct empirical studies to determine to what degree social learning theories and early intervention impact the academic performance of young African-American males.

Taylor (1994) designed three experimental studies to test some of the constructs outlined earlier related to social skills development. Boys from grades 1 and 2 were selected to participate. Experiment #1 assessed the impact of a structured social skills program on academic and interpersonal skills, attendance, and office referrals. Experiment #2 was designed to determine the impact of a structured social skills program on reading and mathematic achievement of boys in grades 1 and 2. Finally, Experiment #3 assessed parents' and teachers' perceptions of the effect of the structured social skills program on the reading, mathematics, and interpersonal skills of boys in the first three grades.

EXPERIMENT #1

Subjects in this study were young African-American boys from a large metropolitan city in the east. Significant improvements were noted in social skills and academic performance along with positive changes in the boys' attitudes toward girls. Hypotheses were constructed to determine whether significant differences existed in reading, mathematics, interpersonal skills, attendance, fewer referrals to the office, and parents' and teachers' perception of social skills development. Major and minor hypotheses were tested. Significant levels were set at the .05 level of confidence.

Major Hypothesis

There will be a significant difference in the academic and interpersonal skills of African-American males after they have participated in a yearlong structured program in social skills development.

Minor Hypothesis

1. There will be a significant difference in reading and math grades of African-American Males after they have participated in a structured social skills program.
2. There will be a significant difference in the attendance and referrals to the office of African-American males after they have participated in a structured social skills program.
3. There will be a significant difference in the way parents and teachers perceive the social skills development of African-American males after participation in the structured social skills program.

Sample

Boys selected to participate in this study were enrolled in grades 1 and 2. The boys were administered a preassessment inventory before the intervention program was initiated by teachers participating in the study. The inventory was not administered to determine who would be selected or rejected to participate. Rather, it was administered to determine the types of social skills development that the boys needed (refer to Appendix B).

Instrumentation

A preassessment inventory was constructed and administered to African-American males who participated in the study. Results from the inventory indicated a variety of social skills deficits such as poor interpersonal skills, stress, poor organization and study skills, and destructive and aggressive behaviors. These deficits formed the basis for developing the structured social skills program and for grouping the boys into various groups for remediating or eliminating the social skills deficits.

A student assessment profile was constructed for teachers to record the boys reading and mathematics grades and social development on a pre/posttest basis.

A social skills checklist was also developed and administered to the boys on a pre/posttest basis by teachers and parents. Forty items in the checklist were rated on a four-point scale ranging from always (a lot, sometimes) to never. Total scores were computed by teachers and parents for each boy involved in the study.

Intervention

Young African-American males who participated in this study were exposed to a year of structured social skills training. Activities included techniques for improving bonding, attention, belonging, recognition of their roles and positions in a group, developing confidence, motivation, caring, problem-solving techniques, and other behavioral problems.

For each skill a set of steps were developed and presented following a set sequence: (1) The teacher modeled the behavior; (2) the student attempted to repeat the demonstrated behavior; (3) other students critiqued the behavior; and (4) the student practiced the skill independent of the group. These steps assisted young Black males in internalizing their behaviors and assessing how their behaviors impact others.

The structured social skills program followed the listed format for each behavior taught:

1. Behaviors were written in behavioral terms.
2. Task analysis was applied until each skill was mastered before moving to the next skill.
3. Some physical arrangements in the classroom were necessary to accomplish some of the skills.
4. No specific time of the school day was devoted to skill training; rather, the training was infused into the regular curriculum whenever possible.
5. A reinforcement system was developed before the intervention was initiated.
6. Specific rules were developed for each skill with as much input from the boys as possible, and written in observable and measurable terms.
7. Rules were understood by the boys; that is, they were able to complete the task.

In selecting skills, emphasis was placed on meeting the personal and social needs of the boys as perceived by them. Once the skills were selected, they were broken down into small manageable tasks (task analysis). New social skills were added only when students had successfully transferred a prior skill.

Analysis of Data

Data were recorded on a student assessment profile. Sum totals for each of the measures in reading, math attendance, office referrals, and social skills development were used in analyzing the data. Several types of analyses were conducted, including descriptive statistics, "t" tests, and Kolmongorow-Smirnow test. Results for all measures were significant beyond the .01 level of confidence. Table 7.1 shows the number of absences between the two testing periods.

Table 7.1
Pre/Post Frequency Analysis of Days Absent (N=33)

No. of Days	No. of Persons Pretest	Percent Pretest	No. of Persons Posttest	Percent Posttest
00	6	18	11	33
01	4	12	4	12
02	3	9	3	9
03	5	15.5	5	15.5
04	5	15.5	3	9
05	4	12	3	9
09	3	9	1	3
10	1	3	2	6.5
11	1	3	1	3
13	0	0	0	0
16	1	3	0	0
20	0	1	0	0
TOTAL:	**33**	**100%**	**33**	**100%**

It is evident from Table 7.1 that the structured social skills training program had a significant impact on attendance. Perfect attendance increased from 18% to 33% by the end of the year. Generally, the boys showed a greater decrease in the number of days absent between the two recording periods. It should also be noted that there was a significant decrease in the number of lower days absent (13-20) between pre- and post-recordings.

The number of office referrals between the two recording periods are summarized in Table 7.2.

Table 7.2
Number and Percent of Office Referrals (*N*=32)

No. of Referrals	Pre- Number	Pre- Percent	Post- Number	Post- Percent
0	29	90.5	31	97
1	2	6.5	1	3
2	1	3.0	0	0
TOTAL:	32	100%	32	100%

Table 7.2 shows the number of referrals between the two recording periods. Some differences can be seen between the number of referrals between the two periods. There was a significant decrease in office referrals between the two periods. During the post-period, 31 (97%) of the boys were not referred to the office compared to 29 (90.5%) during the pre-period. No boys were referred during the post-period more than twice.

Results

Table 7.3 outlines the numbers and percentages of pre/post reading and mathematics grades of young African-American males participating in the study.

Table 7.3
Frequency Analyses of Pre/Post Reading and Mathematics Grades
(N=33)

| | READING | | | | MATHEMATICS | | | |
Grade	Pre- #	Pre- %	Post- #	Post- %	Pre- #	Pre- %	Post- #	Post- %
Good	8	24	13	39	1	3	10	30
Satisfac.	14	42	18	54	12	36	14	36
Unsatis.	5	15	1	3.5	5	15	6	18
Fail	6	49	1	3.5	12	46	3	9
TOTAL:	33	100	33	100	33	100	33	100

Table 7.3 reveals that grades in reading and mathematics improved significantly between the two testing periods. Specifically, there was a significant increase in "Good" grades for both subjects.   The satisfactory categories showed the greatest gains. The unsatisfactory category showed a slight decrease for each measure; similarly, a decrease was noted in the number of failing grades received between the two testing periods.

Chi-square results are reported in Table 7.4 for reading and mathematics achievement.

Table 7.4
Chi-Square Values Pre/Post Achievement
Reading and Mathematics (N=33)

	χ^2	P
Reading	19.8	$).001$
Math	12.8	$).001$

Both reading and mathematics achievement showed a significant difference between the pre- and posttesting periods. Both measures were significant beyond the .001 level. These results imply that the intervention had a positive effect on the reading and mathematics achievement of young African-American males.

Table 7.5 shows the means, standard deviations, and "t" test results for reading and mathematics achievement.

Table 7.5
Means, Standard Deviations, and T-Test Analyses
for Reading and Mathematics Grades

Measures	Pre-Analysis Mean	SD	Post-Analysis Mean	SD	T-Value	P
Reading	3.85	1.004	4.49	1.176	5.60	>.001
Math	2.758	1.323	4.121	1.193	7.22	>.001

Inspection of Tables 7.4 and 7.5 clearly shows that significant differences occurred between the two testing periods in reading and mathematics achievement. The significant level surpassed the .001 level of confidence. These data suggest that the structured social skills program had a significant impact on the reading and mathematic achievement of the young African-American males. Thus, the hypothesis stating that there will be a significant difference in reading and mathematics achievement of African-American males after they had participated in a structured social skills program was supported beyond the .001 level of confidence.

Pre/post perception of the social skills development of the boys participating in the study as viewed by parents and teachers is reflected in Table 7.6 and Table 7.7.

Data in Tables 7.6 and 7.7 strongly suggest significant differences in social skills development as reported by both teachers and parents. Teachers tended to rate social behavior growth higher. Results supported the hypothesis stating that parents and teachers would perceive social skills development of African-American males as positive after they had participated in structured social skills.

The Kolmogorow-Smirnow Statistical Test was used to analyze the impact of the intervention on absences and office referrals. Data are shown in Table 7.8.

The results shown in Table 7.8 support the hypothesis stating that there would be a significant difference in attendance and office referrals of African-American males after they had participated in a structured social skills program. All of the measures were significant beyond the .01 level of confidence.

Perceptions of social skills development as reported by teachers and parents are reflected in Table 7.9.

Table 7.6
Teachers' Perception of Social Skills Development (*N*=28)

PRE-SOCIAL SKILLS		POST-SOCIAL SKILLS	
Score	Number	Score	Number
-48	1	13	1
-59	1	13	1
-65	1	14	1
-67	1	15	1
-68	1	17	1
-75	1	18	1
-76	2	18	1
-77	1	20	1
-78	3	21	1
-79	2	21	1
-81	1	21	1
-83	1	23	1
-85	1	24	1
-88	1	24	1
-91	3	25	4
-92	1	28	1
-93	1	28	1
-95	2	28	1
-97	1	29	2
-100	1	30	1
-106	1	31	4
TOTAL:	28	TOTAL:	28

Table 7.7
Parents' Perception of Social Skills Development (*N*=21)

PRE-SOCIAL SKILLS		POST-SOCIAL SKILLS	
Score	Number	Score	Number
-67	1	31	2
-74	1	29	1
-79	2	28	3
-82	1	27	1
-84	1	26	3
-85	2	25	3
-88	3	23	1
-89	1	24	1
-90	1	22	1
-91	1	21	2
-92	2	20	2
-95	5	18	1
TOTAL:	21	TOTAL:	21

Data in Table 7.9 strongly suggest significant differences in the social skills development as reported by teachers and parents. Significant differences beyond the .01 level were reported for both groups (teachers and parents). Data supported one of the listed hypotheses, which stated that parents and teachers would perceive social skills development of African-American males as positive after they had participated in a structured social skills program.

Significant differences reported in Tables 7.8 and 7.9 strongly supported the major hypothesis of this study: That there would be a significant difference in the academic and interpersonal skills of African-American males after they had participated in a yearlong structured program in social skills development. All measures were significant beyond the .01 level of confidence.

Discussion

Generally, most of the African-American males in this study were pleased with their progress and voiced an interest in continuing with the program. Similarly, both teachers and parents were pleased with the significant social and academic gains that students had made in improving their academic and interpersonal skills.

Table 7.8

Means, Standard Deviations, and Kolmogorow-Smirnow (K-S) Analysis for Absences and Office Referrals (N=33)

	Pre-Measure				Post-Measure			
Measure	Mean	SD	K-S Value	P	Mean	SD	K-S Value	P
Absences	5.121	4.827	0.994	).01	3.667	5.206	1.552	).01
Office Referrals	0.281	0.883	2.933	).01	0.094	0.296	3.086	).01

Table 7.9

Means, Standard Deviations, and Kolmogorow-Smirnow Analysis of Social Skills Development (N=33)

Social Skills	Pre-Social Skills				Post-Social Skills			
	Means	SD	K-S Value	P	Means	SD	K-S Value	P
Parent	87.048	7.553	0.8111	).01	24.952	3.653	0.592	).01
Teacher	81.821	13.024	0.6566	).01	23.500	5.840	0.7633	).01

The findings of this investigation imply that there is a vital need to intervene and teach social skills to African-American males at an early age. Thus, the data tended to support the premise that deficits in social skills development can be compensated for African-American males if early systematic planning is conducted involving both the home and the school.

Recommendations

The project appeared to have changed some of the boys' negative and aggressive behavior, enhanced their self-images, and increased achievement in reading and mathematics. The following recommendations would strengthen the program:

> 1. The total resources of the school should be used and integrated in order to bring about desired changes in behavior.
> 2. Additional studies should be attempted in other schools to see if the results of this study can be replicated.
> 3. Parents must become an integral part of all planning designed to improve the social skills of their children.
> 4. Studies should be designed to follow up on the progress of the project for the boys over a span of three to four years to determine the long-term effect of the structured social skills program on behavior.

EXPERIMENT #2

The study was designed to employ social skills to improve reading and mathematic skills. A structured social skills program was developed for young African-American males in a large urban setting. Thirty-three boys were selected to participate in the study. The boys had previously demonstrated social skills deficits as determined by a preassessment instrument.

The structured social skills program was conducted over a one-year period. Findings indicated that the boys showed significant improvement in interpersonal skills as well as reading and mathematic achievement. All measures were significant at the .01 level or greater; specific recommendations were made for strengthening the program.

Major Hypothesis

There will be a significant difference in the reading, mathematics, and interpersonal skills of young African-American males as viewed by teachers and parents after they have participated in a yearlong structured program in social skills development.

Minor Hypothesis

1. There will be a significant relationship in the reading and math achievement of young African-American males as perceived by teachers and parents after they have participated in a structured social skills program.
2. There will be a significant relationship in how parents and teachers perceive the social skills development of young African-American males after they have participated in a structured interpersonal program.

Sample

As in Experiment #1, boys selected to participate in this study were in grades 1 and 2; teachers and parents of these boys ($N=28$ for both groups) also participated.

Instrumentation

A Likert-type scale was constructed and administered to the teachers and parents on a pre-posttest basis relevant to mathematics, reading, and interpersonal skills. There were 36 items in the instrument, which were rated on a five-point scale ranging from strongly agree to strongly disagree. Total scores were computed.

Intervention

Young African-American males who participated in this study were exposed to a year of structured interpersonal and social skills strategies. The program was designed to determine if social skills training has any impact upon mathematics and reading performance.

The same steps employed for social skills training in Experiment #1 were used in Experiment #2: (1) The teacher modeled the behavior; (2) the student attempted to repeat the demonstrated behavior; (3) other students critiqued the behavior; and (4) the student practiced the skill independent of the group. These steps assisted young Black males in internalizing their behaviors and assessing how their behaviors impacted others.

The structured social skills program followed the listed format for each behavior taught:

1. Behaviors were written in behavioral terms.

2. Task analysis was applied until each skill was mastered before moving to the next skill.

3. Some physical arrangements in the classroom were necessary to accomplish some of the skills.

4. No specific time of the school day was devoted to skill training; rather, the training was infused into the regular curriculum whenever possible.

5. A reinforcement system was developed before the intervention was initiated.

6. Specific rules were developed for each skill with as much input from the boys as possible, and written in observable and measurable terms.

7. Rules were understood by the boys; that is, they were able to complete the task.

New social skills were added only when students had successfully transferred a prior skill.

Mathematics and reading instruction followed the prescribed curriculum. No special technique or innovative strategies were used. The intent of the study was to determine the effects of a structured social skills program on mathematics and reading achievement.

Analysis of Data

Sum totals for each of the measures in reading, math, and social skills development were used in analyzing the data. Several types of analyses were conducted, including Chi-squares and correlations. The Chi-square results were computed for reading and mathematical achievement as well as social skills development to determine significant levels. Significant levels were set at the **.05** level of confidence for all measures. Correlations were computed to show the relationship between the variables on a pre-posttest basis.

Table 7.10 shows how teachers and parents perceived the impact of a structured social skills program on social skills, mathematics, and reading skills.

Data in Table 7.10 clearly show that parents and teachers thought that the structured program in social skills significantly affected the reading, mathematics, and social skills of the boys involved in the study. All measures for the study variables were greater than the **.05** level of confidence. Chi-square results supported the major hypothesis of this study, which stated that there will be a significant difference in the reading, mathematics, and interpersonal skills of young

African-American males as viewed by teachers and parents after they have participated in a structured social skills program.

Table 7.10

Chi-Square Results of Parents' and Teachers' Perceptions of the Impact of the Social Skills Program on Mathematics and Reading Achievement ($N=33$)

VARIABLES	χ^2	P
Social Skills	3.92	$>$.05
Mathematics	4.44	$>$.05
Reading	5.39	$>$.05

Table 7.11

Correlations of Teachers' and Parents' Perceptions of Pre-Posttest Results Between Three Basic Study Variables[1] ($N=33$)

	SOCIAL SKILLS		MATH		READING	
VARIABLES	Teacher	Parent	Teacher	Parent	Teacher	Parent
Social Skills	.38	.24	.70	.23	.51	.22
Math	.63	.51	.74	.47	.76	.50
Reading	.83	.48	.79	.33	.81	.49

Table 7.11 summarizes the correlations of teachers' and parents' view of the study's variables.

---

[1] All correlations were significant at the .05 level of confidence or higher.

Correlations were computed to determine if significant relationship existed between the perceptions of teachers and parents toward the study variables. All variables correlated significantly. Data suggested that both teachers and parents agreed that the training program had a significant impact on the boys in the areas of reading, mathematics, and social skills development.

These data support the minor hypotheses of this study:

Hypothesis #1. There will be significant relationship in the reading, mathematics of young African-American males as perceived by teachers and parents after they have participated in a structured social skills program.

Hypothesis #2. There will be a significant relationship in how parents and teachers perceive the social skills development of young African-American males after they have participated in a structured interpersonal program.

Discussion

Thus, there were significant agreements among and between the groups relevant to the benefits of the program. Results of this study clearly showed that parents and teachers overwhelmingly viewed the structured program in interpersonal skills as highly successful. Additionally, the program appeared to have improved communication between the teachers and parents. They worked cooperatively for the benefit of the boys. For example, a significant number of parents volunteered to work in the structured program.

Not only did the boys show significant improvement in reading and mathematics. They also showed significant improvement in social skills. Near the conclusion of the program, boys were observed using appropriate manners, following school and classroom rules, coming to school on time, being less tardiness, and showing respect for girls and adult authorities.

Recommendations

Both teachers and parents gave high praise for the program and recommended that it become part of the regular curriculum. Specific recommendations include:

1. Parents should be encouraged to participate frequently in school activities.
2. Additional activities of this nature should be jointly planned by teachers and parents.

3. Parents should be given specific information relevant to improving social skills.

4. Follow- up studies should be conducted over a span
of years to determine the long-term effects of social
training.

EXPERIMENT #3

Experiment #3 was designed to determine parents' and teachers'
perceptions of the use of a structured social skills program to improve
the reading, mathematics, and interpersonal achievement of young
African-American males. The structured social skills program, as in
Experiments #1 and #2, was conducted over a one-year period.
Findings indicated that the boys showed significant improvement in
reading, mathematics, and interpersonal skills.

Major Hypothesis

There will be a significant difference in the reading, mathematics,
and interpersonal skills of young African-American males after they
have participated in a yearlong structured program in social skills
development.

Minor Hypothesis

1. There will be a significant difference in the reading
and mathematics achievement of young African-
American males after they have participated in a
structured social skills program.

2. There will be a significant difference in the way
parents and teachers perceive the social skills development of young African-American males after they
have participated in a structured social skills program.

Methods and Procedures

Methods and procedures identical to those employed in Experiments
#1 and #2 used. The one exception was the grade level of the boys
who participated. Thirty-three boys in three first grades were selected
to participate.

Analysis of Data

Data were recorded on a student assessment profile. Sum totals for each of the measures in reading, mathematics, and social skills development were used in analyzing the data. Several types of analyses were conducted, including descriptive statistics and the "t" test. The "t" test results were computed for reading and mathematical grades as well as to determine significant levels on other measures. Significant levels were set at the .05 level of confidence for all measures.

Results

Table 7.12 outlines "t" test values of pre/post reading and mathematics grades of African-American males participating in the study.

Table 7.12

Means, Standard Deviations, and T-Test Analyses for Reading and Mathematics Achievement

Measure	Pre-Analysis		Post-Analysis		T-Value	P
	Mean	SD	Mean	SD		
Reading	3.67	1.02	4.61	1.172	5.60	).001
Math	2.56	1.321	4.13	1.193	7.22	).001

Inspection of Table 7.12 clearly shows that significant differences occurred between the two periods (pre/post) in reading and mathematics achievement. The significant level surpassed the .001 level of confidence. Data suggest that the structured social skills program had a significant impact on the reading and mathematics achievement of the young African-American males. Thus, the hypothesis stating that there will be a significant difference in the reading and mathematics achievement of African-American males after they have participated in a structured social skills program was supported beyond the .001 level of confidence.

Pre/post perceptions of the social skills development of boys participating in the study as viewed by parents and teachers are reflected in Tables 7.13 and 7.14.

Data in Tables 7.13 and 7.14 strongly suggest that significant differences existed in the social skills development as reported by teachers and parents. Significant percent differences were reported by both teachers and parents. Teachers tended to rate social behavior growth higher. Results supported the hypothesis stating that parents and teachers would perceive the social skills development of African-American males as positive after they had participated in a structured social skills program.

Significant differences reported in Tables 7.13 and 7.14 strongly supported the major hypothesis of this study. That there will be a significant difference in the reading and mathematic achievement of African-American males after they have participated in a yearlong structured program in social skills development. All measures were significant beyond the .01 level of confidence.

Table 7.13

Parents' Perception of Social Skills Development (N=21)

Pre-Social Skills		Post-Social Skills	
Score	Number	Score	Number
-69	1	30	2
-76	1	33	1
-82	2	34	3
-86	1	30	1
-80	1	31	1
-88	2	29	3
-93	3	25	1
-86	1	23	1
-95	1	20	1
-86	1	19	2
-93	2	18	2
-91	5	16	1
TOTAL: 21		TOTAL:	21

Discussion

Generally, most of the African-American males in this study were pleased with their progress and voiced an interest in continuing with the program. Both teachers and parents were also pleased with the significant social and academic gains that students had made.

This study, based on the findings of this investigation, implies that there is a vital need to intervene and teach social skills to young African-American males at an early age. Data from this study tended to support the premise that deficits in social skills development can be compensated for young African-American males if early systematic planning is conducted between the home and school.

In analyzing the statistical data as to the project's effectiveness, there is a need to proceed cautiously, however. Deficiencies in the research design involved a failure to determine actual achievement in reading and mathematics, attitudes toward school, length of time of the project in the school. In addition, involvement of the school in other experimental programs may have added to and impacted the positive results. Nevertheless, the project appeared to have significantly changed the negative and aggressive behaviors of the boys, expanded self-images, and increased achievement in reading and mathematics. Improvement is needed if the program is to be strengthened; thus, the following recommendations are made:

1. The total resources of the school should be used and integrated in order to bring about desired changes in behavior.

2. Additional studies should be attempted in other schools to see if the results of this study can be replicated.

3. Parents must become an integral part of all planning designed to improve social skills of their children.

4. Studies should be designed to follow up on the progress of the project and study the boys over a span of three or four years to determine the long-term effect of the structured social skills program on behavior.

Table 7.14

Teachers' Perception of Social Skills Development (*N*=28)

Pre-Social Skills			Post-Social Skills	
Score	Number		Score	Number
-51	1		15	1
-61	1		12	1
-63	1		11	1
-65	1		16	1
-62	1		19	1
-77	1		21	1
-74	2		19	1
-78	1		21	1
-80	3		23	1
-81	2		20	1
-83	1		19	1
-85	1		25	1
-87	1		27	1
-89	1		23	1
-93	3		30	4
-96	1		31	1
-95	1		33	1
-98	2		32	1
-99	1		31	2
-87	1		34	1
-102	1		35	4
TOTAL:	**28**		**TOTAL:**	**28**

SUMMARY

Three experimental studies were conducted to determine the impact of a structured social skills program on academic and interpersonal skills, attendance, and office referrals of African-American males in grades 1 and 2. All of the boys participated in a yearlong structured social skills training program. All measures showed significant growth between pre- and posttesting. These studies add to the increasing body of knowledge related to the value of systematically teaching social skills to young African-American males. Data suggest that deficits in social skills development can be compensated for if intervention is attempted early.

8

Social/Interpersonal Skills Curriculum for Young African-American Males

CURRICULUM DEVELOPMENT: AN OVERVIEW

Curriculum development is designed to reflect the course of study in schools. It is intended to present information to students in an organized manner through various instructional methods and strategies. Teachers must be cognizant of creative and innovative ways to individualize and maximize learning for pupils by providing practical learning activities (Beane, 1990; Kristo, 1982; Ross, 1993; Gruenewald, 1990).

According to Beane, et al (Beane, 1993; Dodge, 1988; Hedley, 1990), designing curriculum involves two major methodologies. The first methodology is experimental instruction. *Experimental instruction* is designed to intrinsically motivate student interests inside and outside of the classroom. The second approach, systematic instruction, involves teacher/student interaction. The major purpose of *systematic instruction* is to develop a skill or concept and design materials and activities that enable students to achieve the selected objectives.

Curriculum development in most school districts is concerned with developing academics in order to equip pupils to master the complex tasks presented by our society. This approach is valid for most pupils. However, due to poor social and interpersonal skills development of many minority and young African-American males, social skill development may be necessary before academic skills can be mastered.

It is generally agreed by most professionals in the field of education that schools should be involved in teaching social and interpersonal skills. For example, social skills education and interpersonal skills development are ideal ways to teach responsibility for self and others and for exploring the meaning of human interaction and relationships.

The subject is too important and complex for the home to handle alone.

A social skills curriculum can also help students understand: (1) how to develop self-esteem along with their emotions and how their emotions affects others; (2) how to develop positive social relation-ships; (3) respect for others; (4) respect for rules and regulations; (5) ways to develop moral and character; (6) ways to examine one's values; (7) ways to make responsible choices; (8) their potential and worth as human beings; (9) How to develop a sense of responsibility toward others and ways of behaving appropriately in public places; (10) the role and duty of responsible citizens; and (11) how to develop effective communication skills.

Curriculum strategies outlined in this text are designed to address the social skills and others as they relate specifically to young African-American males. Experimental, direct, and systematic curriculum methodologies will be employed.

The phenomenon of educating African-American school-age males has been studied and investigated extensively, resulting in numerous educators advocating that these "special" young males demonstrate inappropriate social skills/behaviors inside as well as outside the classroom. Developing the appropriate social skills for successful interaction with peers and significant adults (teachers, parents) can be considered one of the most important accomplishments of childhood and early adolescence should be addressed as soon as possible. This is particularly true in the area of establishing and maintaining relations with peers and authority figures. Not only can social skills deficits have a negative impact on future interpersonal functioning, it may also affect current functioning, reducing the quality and quantity of the learning experiences to which students are exposed in their educational settings (Furnham, 1986).

Social skills have been defined as goal-oriented, rule-governed, situation-specific learned behaviors that vary according to social context. Social skills involving both observable and nonobservable cognitive and affective elements that help elicit positive or neutral responses and avoid negative responses from others (Brody, 1977; Collins, 1992; DiMartino, 1990; Dorr-Bremme, 1992; Furnham, 1986). As such, social behavior constitutes an intricate interfactional process. As a result, the behavior of school-age children influences and is influenced by that of their partners (e.g., teachers, mentors, tutors, and peers) within the interaction.

Society expects that when children reach various developmental stages, they will demonstrate greater foresight and more controlled behaviors. Society also expects that children will be capable, not only of meeting increased demands within learning tasks, but also more complex, subtle social situations. Failure to meet these expectations may increase their sense of social alienation and helplessness.

The curriculum presented here is designed to enable young African-American males to become socially contributing members of society by meeting expected standards. Strategies have been developed to assist educators in providing these students appropriate social skills training to enable them to operate successfully in the schools and society. Intervention techniques have been selected based upon research techniques to assist young Black males in controlling aggression, assuming responsibility, and becoming productive members of the group.

The author highly endorses that proactive approach be employed when teaching social skills to young African-American males. Since proactive instruction provides children with social intervention before negative behaviors occur, this approach is preferable to reactive teaching. Whereas proactive instruction teaches social skills before social rejection is experienced, reactive instruction waits for the individual to fail and then applies intervention strategies. Many young African-American males have problems developing appropriate social skills due to the problems outlined throughout the text. Proactive instruction will prevent many of the negative consequences of inappropriate social skills, as well as improve the self-image of young African-American males. Recommended strategies for proactive instruction may assist the boys in:

1. dealing positively with accusations
2. accepting the feelings of others in a nonthreatening manner
3. respecting the feelings of others
4. avoiding fights and conflicts
5. dealing effectively with teasing
6. giving praise or compliments to others
7. accepting compliments from others
8. apologizing for inappropriate behavior
9. expressing anger in a positive way
10. showing affection and appreciation toward others
11. practicing self-control

These instructional activities may be expanded or modified as needed.

As indicated throughout this book, young African-American males must be taught appropriate social skills if they are going to be contributing members of society. The social skills outlined here should be infused throughout the curriculum and integrated as needed by the teacher. These strategies are seen as immediate, useful resources for teaching pro-social skills to young African-American males. It is a how-to-do guide, providing specific examples and strategies for teachers and other professionals. Additionally, the curriculum is based upon indepth research and years of teaching and observing the social skills development of young African-American males.

A FUNCTIONAL APPROACH

A functional approach to teaching social skills to young African-American males can easily be infused throughout the curriculum. A functional approach involves exposing the learner to real-life situations, concepts, and activities such as self-identity, acquiring self-concept, achieving socially acceptable behavior, bonding, respecting the rights of others, maintaining good interpersonal skills, achieving independence, employing problem-solving skills, taking turns, and communicating appropriately with others.

Several group activities, such as role playing, modeling, and cooperative groups may be used to teach social skills to young African-American males from a functional and holistic viewpoint within the context of real-life experiences. In essence, children are taught to model, imitate, and demonstrate appropriate social skills in the reality in which they exist (McGinnis & Goldstein, 1984).

CURRICULUM DEVELOPMENT

A social skills curriculum should be based upon those social skills needed to function successfully in one's society. Much of the research reviewed indicates that a significant number of young African-American males have not mastered the social skills needed to function successfully in our society (Gibbs, 1991; Holland, 1993; Obiakor, 1990; Taylor, 1993; Hilliard, 1988).

The initial step in developing a social skills curriculum is to identify those general social behaviors that are critical to successful social functioning. These general social behaviors are then rewritten as general objectives, which provide the framework for constructing other components of the curriculum.

The second stage is to sequence specific objectives as they relate to the general objectives. All specific objectives are designed to achieve the general objectives. Specific objectives are stated in behavioral and measurable terms. The third step is to identify activities and resources that can achieve the stated objectives. (Refer to Appendix F for selected resources). Activities should be functional and reflect real-life experiences that young African-American males are exposed to.

As much as possible, parents should be involved in reinforcing the social skills taught. Parents may be used as resource individuals and may offer suggestions relative to material and activities. (See Chapter 6 for specific strategies for involving parents.)

The fourth step is to include cultural, ethnic, and racial diversity into the curriculum. This approach affords young African-American males the opportunity to appreciate and understand their own self-worth and sense of importance and belonging as well as identify Blacks and other minorities who have made significant contributions in several fields. An additional benefit is that the young Black males can identify and associate with appropriate role models.

A curriculum that does not highlight the contributions of Blacks and minorities gives an inaccurate and distorted view of the many significant contributions made by them. Multicultural activities and strategies enriches the curriculum by showing differences in cultural styles, patterns, and interests of diverse groups.

ASSESSMENT OF SOCIAL SKILLS

Assessment is long-term and continuous. This process is designed to monitor how effectively a strategy is achieving a desired goal. Both self-monitoring by students and teacher monitoring are recommended. Most students welcome the opportunity to be involved in monitoring their own progress toward attaining a skill. Chapter 4 overviews selected social assessment techniques.

SOCIAL SKILLS UNIT

General Objective No. 1 of the Unit:
Young African-American males will achieve socially acceptable behaviors in social and interpersonal situations.

Specific Objectives:
A. The boys will respect members of the opposite sex.
B. The boys will demonstrate appropriate character traits needed for acceptance in the public.
C. The boys will demonstrate proper behavior in public places.
D. The boys will show respect for the rights and properties of others.
E. The boys will recognize authority and follow instructions of school, home, and the community.
F. The boys will recognize personal roles in public places.
G. The boys will use terms such as "please," "thank you," and "excuse me" at the appropriate times and places.

H. The boys will practice sportsmanship by sharing toys and information.
I. The boys will stand in line without bothering others.
J. Given a description of behavior on the bus, the boys will show appropriate behavior.
K. The boys will know how and when to give and accept apologies.

Recommended Activities: (individualize and expand as needed)
A. The boys will respect members of the opposite sex.
> 1. Role play a variety of situations showing the boys how to show respect for females.
> 2. During everyday activities and conversations, require the boys to say "please," "thank you, "and "excuse me" to the girls.
> 3. If the boys curse at or call the girls derogatory names, try to distract them. Intervene by defining the word or words, and indicate that these are words that hurt people.
> 4. Show the boys pictures of children working and playing together; point out that both boys and girls are playing and working together and that both sexes are respecting each other.
> 5. Reward the boys when they show appropriate behavior toward girls.
> 6. Assign girls and boys to group activities. Assign equal responsibilities to girls.

B. The boys will demonstrate appropriate character traits and behaviors needed for acceptance in the public.
> 1. Provide activities that the boys require to assist in structured activities.
> 2. Demonstrate to the boys how to move in crowds by saying "excuse me," "pardon me," when people are blocking the way.
> 3. Model appropriate behavior when meeting new people and in all activities where the boys come in contact with the public.
> 4. Explain and demonstrate to students how to observe safety rules and how to be very considerate of others when using public transportation.
> 5. Role play a variety of situations that might occur when the boys are using public transportation. Demonstrate socially acceptable behaviors in these situations.

6. Demonstrate, show films, and model appropriate behaviors for the boys to demonstrate when receiving services from the barber shop, banks, stores, or any other public places.

7. Role play a variety of situations where the boys demonstrate appropriate behavior when receiving public service.

8. Show the boys how to greet people in a socially acceptable language in public.

C. Repeat steps 1 through 8 in section B.

D. The boys will show respect for the rights and properties of others.

1. Provide activities where the boys have to protect and share others properties.

2. Role play activities where the boys are required to cooperate with others for the success and welfare of the group.

3. Initiate a variety of games and activities that require the boys to share or take turns.

4. Provide activities for the boys to share games and discuss the importance of protecting others' properties.

5. Allow time for the boys to bring their games to school to share with the class. Emphasize the importance of safeguarding personal property.

6. Discuss vandalism. Draw from the experiences of the boys. Discuss the legal aspects of vandalism in terms that the boys can understand.

7. Provide activities where the boys verbally compliment their classmates.

E. The boys will recognize authority and follow instructions at school, home, and the community.

1. Through films, videotapes, and demonstrations, show the boys how to respond appropriately to authority and establish rules, supervised and unsupervised. Have the boys narrate or draw appropriate ways of responding to authority.

2. Provide time for boys to share with the class appropriate ways of responding to authorities.

3. Discuss the importance of rules and laws. Summarize the importance of classroom rules. What purpose do they serve and why is it important to obey them?

4. Plan an activity where a rule is broken. Have the boys discuss the consequences of breaking the rule. Discuss how it affects others. List the consequences of the behavior.

5. When the boys break a rule, explain the consequences and demonstrate alternate ways of solving or addressing the problem.

6. Invite a law enforcement officer to speak to the boys. Encourage interaction between the boys and the officer.

7. Encourage parents to establish rules at home for the boys to follow and discuss the consequences of breaking rules.

8. Role play and show films where individuals break laws and are held responsible for their actions. Discuss alternative ways of responding to the situations.

F. The boys will recognize personal roles in public places.

1. Read the boys stories of high interest in which the characters accept responsibilities for their behaviors.

2. Role play a variety of conditions in which the boys are required to make decisions; both appropriate and inappropriate.

3. When a situation arises where the boys have broken a rule, discuss the consequences of such behavior. When possible, involve the boys in selecting the consequences.

4. Develop activities stressing that when one acts inappropriately, one must accept the consequences of the behavior.

5. Encourage the boys to think about the outcomes of their behaviors by providing situations in which they must make choices.

G. The boys will use terms such as "please," "thank you," and "excuse me," at appropriate times.

1. During everyday activities, infuse conversations where the boys will use terms such as "excuse me," "thank you," etc., at appropriate times. Reward the boys for positive responses.

2. Role play a variety of situations requiring courteous responses from the boys.

3. Encourage the boys to use good manners as consumers, through demonstrations and dramatic everyday activities.

4. Provide activities where the boys are required to model behaviors. Praise successful attempts and discuss why others are not successful.

5. Demonstrate to the boys how to move through crowds by saying "excuse me," "may I please pass?," etc.

H. The boys will practice sportsmanship by sharing toys and information.

1. As the boys play and work together, provide activities where they must take turns and share materials. Praise the boys when their attempts are successful.

2. Discuss the concept of "a good sport." Encourage the boys to accept success and failure in sports and games. Praise the boys for being a "good sport," a "good loser" as well as a "good winner."

3. In the school, infuse activities within the curriculum that require that the boys take turns, such as dramatic play activities that can only be successfully completed through teamwork ad cooperation.

4. When the boys lose, encourage them to try again. Discuss the idea that losing is a part of winning. Provide activities that allow the boys to win sometimes.

I. The boys will stand in line without bothering others.

1. Model and demonstrate appropriate behavior while in line. Praise and reward the boys for appropriate behavior.

2. Role play situations where the boys show appropriate behavior in line.

3. Discuss the importance of following rules. Relate how appropriately standing in line is obeying rules.

4. Demonstrate to the boys how standing in line without bothering others is respecting the rights of others.

5. Relate showing appropriate behavior in line to "good citizenship."

J. Given a description of behavior on the bus, the boys will show appropriate behavior.

1. Provide appropriate models for the boys to follow when riding on buses.

2. Demonstrate how to handle situations such as pushing, stepping on toes, loud language, etc., while riding on buses.

3. Role play a variety of situations, appropriate and inappropriate, while riding on the bus.

4. Review films and filmstrips showing appropriate and inappropriate behaviors and have the boys evaluate both types of situations and provide alternative solutions.

K. The boys will know how and when to use rational processes to check their emotions.

1. After a fight or disturbance, form a circle and play a game before discussing the incident.
2. Sing a favorite song with the boys before trying to settle an issue.

General Objective No. 2 of the Unit:
Young African-American males will show positive self-concepts when dealing with others.

Specific Objectives:
A. The boys will know how and when to use rational processes to evaluate their emotions.
B. The boys will emphasize their special uniqueness by recognizing their potential.
C. The boys will recognize the impact of their behavior on others.
D. The boys will personally and positively interact with each other.
E. The boys will show how they can reduce negative repercussions in the classroom.
F. Have the boys to demonstrate special traits of each other.
G. The boys will demonstrate and model behaviors that will enhance their self-image and concepts.
H. Have the boys demonstrate and discuss ways that they can effectively deal with their fears.

Recommended Activities: (individualize and expand as needed)
A. The boys will know how and when to use rational processes to evaluate their emotions.

1. Have the boys choose an attitude they would like to make into an attitude mask: angry, happy, sad, tired, bored, scared, sick; encourage a large variety of feelings. Provide materials for the boys to make the masks. While they are making the masks, ask them to be thinking about how their mask will "act" after completion; have them share with each other.
2. Choose both positive and negative feelings masks to role play each situation.
3. Have the boys identify the major emotions felt most of the time: happy, sad, angry, scared, and tired. Have

them associate a color with each of the emotions. Use mobiles when identifying the boys' emotions.

4. Have the boys to identify people being angry from pictures. Discuss the following:

    a. Why is this person angry?

    b. Have you ever been angry?

    c. What makes you really, really, really angry?

    d. What do you do when you get angry?

5. Discuss some ways to handle anger. Categorize and list on chart paper. Praise the boys for controlling anger in the classroom.

6. Assign boys the task of interviewing a significant other about a problem he had and how it was solved. Films that focus on a central character with a problem to solve serve as good models for the boys and are catalysts for class discussion. The boys should first discuss their problems in small groups. Teammates can then contribute ideas for resolution as well as just being supportive.

7. Teach the following problem-solving steps to the boys:

    a. What is the problem?

    b. Think of solutions.

    c. Select the two or three preferred solutions.

    d. What might happen if they were chosen?

    e. Choose the best solution after reviewing the consequences.

    f. Make a plan.

    g. Do it!

8. Write down messages that can be disruptive to a class environment. This exercise assists the boys in recognizing how deadly put-downs are to others' feelings. It also helps them find ways to change negative responses to more positive ones.

9. Divide the boys into teams. Have the boys make a set of 10 index cards for each team. Instruct them to write a different negative statement on each card. Each team selects one boy to be the dealer who passes out the cards. Each team member reads one put-down message to the group. After each reading, the team

gives messages that could be said instead. The team chooses the best answer to each put-down statement and records them on chart paper.

10. Provide activities for group discussion by showing a picture of emotions taking control. Have the boys give alternative ways to solve the problem.

B. The boys will emphasize their special uniqueness by recognizing their potential.

1. Tell the boys that they are going to be learning about a very special person. Who IS the most special person in the whole world? When a boy comes up with the answer that he is the most special person in the world, praise the boy.

2. Show the boys a stuffed animal with a price tag. "How much are YOU worth?" Discuss with the boys that they are PRICELESS. You are worth more than all the stuffed animals in the world.

3. A circle is formed and an objective is passed around. Each boy is instructed to say something positive about the boy passing the object to him.

4. Have the boys draw pictures about things that they can do successfully. Emphasize the point that all of us have the potential for being successful.

5. Instruct the boys to keep records of their achievements. As they accomplish each of their achievements, they are written down or drawn. The teacher periodically inspects and evaluates the record, making appropriate positive remarks.

6. Encourage the boys to think about things they like about themselves and things they wish they could change. Remind them that there are some things we can change and other things that we cannot change. Discuss with the boys things they can and cannot change.

7. Construct mobiles that have silhouettes of the boys as the center. From the silhouettes, hang words, magazine cut-outs, or drawings that illustrate the various "specialties" of the boys. The boys' name will appear in big letters on the silhouettes.

C. The boys will recognize the impact of their behaviors on others.

1. Use a hand puppet to demonstrate how negative behaviors, such as saying unkind words to others, can have a negative impact on them.

2. Discuss with the boys how they can choose to treat others in a positive way. Pictures or puppets may be used.

3. Group the boys in a circle and have them relate how other people's behaviors have had a negative impact upon them. Solicit solutions from the boys as to how these behaviors can be changed to positive ones.

4. Use creative dramatics and role playing showing how the negative impact of behaviors displayed by others can have an impact on them.

5. Provide activities and examples to assist the boys in internalizing their behaviors, such as thinking out loud before acting and examining the consequences of their behaviors on others.

6. Role play activities showing fair and unfair treatment of others. Outline how unfair treatment may become fair.

D. Provide activities for the boys to interact positively with each other.

1. For each hour of the clock, have the boys fill in a different classmate's name. Encourage them to initiate the meeting with the classmate by introducing themselves. Model to the boys how to make appropriate introductions.

2. Write each boy's name on a slip of paper and put all slips into a small container. As the container is passed, each boy draws the name of another boy and says what is special about him. No negative comments are allowed. This activity requires a great deal of time to complete.

3. Choose a boy to be the recipient of the greeting for the day. Each boy writes a compliment to the chosen person. At the end of the day, the recipient collects all the messages from the class.

4. Encourage the boys to write messages to a peer on special occasions.

5. Have each boy find a special character in a magazine. Give the character a name, place and date of birth, family, friends, and occupation. Have the boys describe how his special person feels.

E. Demonstrate ways that the boys can reduce negative repercussions in the classroom.

1. Provide scenarios for the boys to discuss and role play negative behaviors such as:

a. Suppose that by telling your friend you are angry with him, he becomes angry with you? Stress the fact that frequently holding feelings inside may avoid conflicts.

b. If someone called you ugly or stupid, how would you react? How would you control your feelings?

c. Suppose someone said, "I hate you; get out of my way!"

d. Suppose someone said, "I don't like you."

e. Suppose someone calls you stupid.

2. Provide opportunities for the boys to be involved in constructing classroom rules as well as the consequences for violating the rules.

3. Demonstrate to the boys that all of us at times have many feelings; some that we can control and others that get out of control. Today we are going to discuss ways we can reduce negative feelings inside of us.

4. Use a hand puppet. Make the puppet look shy, scared, happy, and sad. The puppet should elicit empathy from the boys as they identify with some of the puppet's feelings. Have the boys discuss how they would handle their feelings.

F. Provide activities showing special traits of the boys.

1. Give each boy a piece of paper; the pieces of paper are divided into squares. Have them draw and past pictures, photographs, and souvenirs about who he is. When all the squares are completed, they can be taped together and displayed as a scrapbook.

2. Instruct the boys to complete a promotional piece (poem, story, picture, etc.) about themselves.

3. Have promotional information shared with the class in order that they can affirm themselves in front of others.

4. Provide opportunities for the boys to share information about themselves. Use the shared information to determine things that the boys have in common. Have the information shared with the class. This activity may assist in developing the self-concept of shy boys.

5. Videotape the boys performing positive behaviors. Show the tape to the class and accent the positive behaviors.

6. Develop a Citizen of the Week Award. Give certificates to the boys who meet the established criteria.

G. Demonstrate, plan, and model behaviors that enhance the self-images and concepts of the boys.

1. Help students develop an accurate self-description by modeling acceptable behaviors.

2. Model behaviors showing the boys how not to be oversensitive to criticism.

3. Plan activities that assist the boys in clarifying or thinking more about themselves, such as showing photographs and telling stories about themselves.

4. Give examples of how the boys can make positive statements about self and others.

5. Provide opportunities for the boys to discover major sources of influence upon self.

6. Make tokens to give out to boys who have been "caught doing something good."

7. Construct a mobile and hang from it words and phrases that are used in your classroom to promote positive behaviors such as:

"Thank You"	"Excuse Me"
"Good Morning"	"I Like You"
"I Forgive You"	"May I Help?"
"I'm Sorry"	"Can I Help?"

H. Demonstrate and discuss ways that the boys can effectively deal with their fears.

1. Structure group activities where the boys can discuss their fears. Emphasize the fact that all of us have fears at one time or another.

2. Using chart paper, make a list of some of the fears stated by the boys. Discuss ways of minimizing fears.

3. Have the boys use pictures to discuss the types of fears shown and what can be done to reduce the levels of fear.

4. Develop dramatic activities showing how fear may be reduced in the following areas:

a. Someone making fun of you

b. Being left out of an important activity or event

c. Parents divorcing

d. Presenting before a group or the class

e. Afraid of making a mistake

f. Being criticized

g. Moving to another community.
5. Write and develop stories about fears, indicating a solution for controlling them.
6. Have the boys share some of their past fears with the class and explain how they overcame them.

General Objective No. 3 of the Unit:
Young African-American males will identify and evaluate their feelings about others.

Specific Objectives:
A. The boys will realize that other people have feelings and understanding what can be done to help them feel better about themselves.
B. The boys will be made aware of how their anger can affect the feelings and well-being of others.
C. The boys will demonstrate activities showing the impact of negative behaviors on self and others.
D. Have the boys demonstrate the value of accepting praise.
E. The boys will show how to effectively identify and appropriately express their emotions and attitudes.
F. Have the boys emphasize that it is important to discuss their fears with someone who can assist them.
G. Have the boys to assess and evaluate the various types of feelings shown in pictures and films.
H. The boys will show feelings of sympathy and goodwill toward others.

Recommended Activities: (individualize and expand as needed)
A. Assist the boys in realizing that other people have feelings and what can be done to help people feel better about themselves.
1. Show pictures of a person feeling sad and/or scared. Why is this person sad? What do you think happened to her/him? What could he/she do to change those scary, sad feelings?
2. Through pictures, show and emphasize that not everyone is afraid of the same things. Individuals express different feelings toward different things.
3. Discuss with the boys the fact that we have all experienced times when we have so many feelings inside us at the same time that we feel like we cannot handle them. We can control some of our feelings.
4. Instruct the boys that the use of negative phrases and words such as "shut up," "you're stupid," "go

away," "get out of here," and "leave me alone" do not make people feel good about themselves.

5. Use puppets to show different feelings. Post the following questions to the boys:

    a. How did the puppet choose to act out his feelings the first time?

    b. How did he act the second time? Why? Just like we choose our eating habits, we also choose our feelings. We can choose to feel good about ourselves, or we can choose to feel bad about ourselves. We can choose to treat people in positive ways when we express our feelings, or we can choose to handle situations in a negative manner and keep all our feelings inside. Which is easier: letting our feelings out in a positive way or keeping them in? Which is healthier?

B. Make the boys aware of how their anger can affect the feelings and well-being of others.

1. Discuss incidents of angry behaviors in groups, highlighting how the angry behaviors affected others in the group.

2. Show pictures of angry expressions. Discuss how other means of expressing anger could be used.

3. Using pictures, films, stories, etc., have the boys discuss what might have caused the anger. How could the incident have been prevented?

4. Teach the boys techniques that enable them to control their anger, such as being sensitive to feedback and evaluating their behaviors.

5. Instruct the boys on how anger is manifested. Highlight the physical and social aspects.

6. Using role playing and creative dramatics to demonstrate various stages of anger. Discuss alternate ways of expressing anger.

7. Develop short stories and plays showing how anger can be expressed in a positive fashion.

8. Model various stages of anger for the boys along with techniques for controlling it.

C. Provide activities showing the impact of negative behaviors on self and others.

1. Discuss with the boys how negative behaviors impact others.

2. Through the use of pictures, discuss how negative behaviors are influencing the characters in the pictures.

3. Have the boys role play negative behaviors, reflecting their impact on others.

4. Develop short skits with the boys portraying how negative behaviors influence others.

5. Using a variety of media, art, painting, etc., have the boys develop stories displaying the consequences of negative behaviors on oneself and others.

6. Use puppets to show the negative impact of behaviors on others. Ask the boys how they feel about themselves when they are happy? sad? mad? Use the puppets to demonstrate the behaviors boys would like to show.

7. Say something unkind to the puppet; have it sit up tall and shake his/her head "no" as if to refuse to accept the negative remark.

D. Demonstrate to the boys the value of accepting praise.

1. Role play incidents showing the boys how not to be uncomfortable with praise.

2. Discuss with the boys how not to become embarrassed when accepting praise.

3. Review films and videotapes showing males accepting praise.

4. Model appropriate behaviors for accepting praise.

5. Have the boys share their experiences in accepting praise.

6. Model appropriate behavior showing the boys how to apologize.

7. Praise the boys when they have accomplished a positive task or displayed positive behaviors.

E. Develop strategies for effectively identifying and appropriately expressing emotions and attitudes.

1. Discuss with the boys how what they feel affects the way they behave. Use the puppets to help illustrate. Have the boys identify the puppets' feelings by demonstrating various moods. Ask the boys to demonstrate when they are glad, angry, or sad.

2. Make a booklet for each boy. Make a special key for each booklet so the boys can readily recognize their booklet. Review the keys frequently with the boys

until they can remember them. Have the boys write the secret feelings or feelings that are very special to them inside their booklets and lock them up to keep them safe.

3. Have the boys look through magazines. Find pictures of people who have great smiles. Cut out the smiles and paste them on the cover of books. Now look at the cover. How does it make you feel?

4. Ask the boys to articulate their feelings and listen to the feelings of others during story and sharing time. Elicit criticism from the class.

5. Create scenarios expressing emotions and attitudes. Scenarios should be both negative and positive. Have the boys group and classify the scenarios based on how they would act.

6. Using the information from #5, have the boys draw pictures. Discuss and critique each picture.

F. Emphasize to the boys that it is important to discuss their fears with someone who can assist them.

1. List and categorize fears with the boys. Stress the fact that fears are often a result of our perceptions of a situation, rather than the danger being inherent in the situation. Instruct the boys to discuss their fears with parents, pastor, counselor, relatives, and close friends. Ask them to seek their opinions and advice.

2. Ask the boys to discuss their fears. Encourage them to explain and identify what the fears are. Provide suggestions for dealing with the fears.

3. Relate to the boys that most fears are imaginary. Have the boys write their fears on a piece of paper and place them in a paper bag. Pull fears from the bag and separate real fears from imaginary fears. Discuss both types of fears.

4. Use puppets to demonstrate various stages of imaginary fears.

5. From the list of fears in #1, discuss with the boys how these fears may be minimized or corrected.

6. Role play how fears originate and how many of them are based upon uncertainties, doubts, rumors, and untruths.

7. Discuss with the boys and demonstrate how some fears are needed and useful.

G. Show pictures, films, and videotapes and model behaviors about individuals expressing feelings. Provide opportunities for the boys to assess and evaluate the various types of feelings.

1. Collect magazine pictures of people's faces expressing different feelings: surprise, contentment, anxiety, anger, grief, etc. Have the boys study the pictures and decide the circumstances that led to the emotion shown. This technique may be used individually or in groups.

2. Emphasize the importance of feelings by stressing that feelings make our lives rich and exciting, but that they can cause us problems depending upon how we act on those feelings as well as how we deal with them.

3. Instruct the boys to reflect about things they feel good about in others and compare to their own feelings.

4. Develop cooperative groups. Have the boys role play certain feelings such as sad, happy, upset, disagreeing, and agreeing. Have other groups critique the feelings and give alternative ways they would have dealt with their feelings.

5. Review films and videotapes where people express different feelings. Have the boys group and classify them.

6. Write stories expressing different feelings. Have the boys share with the class.

H. Instruct the boys that it is okay to show feelings, sympathy, and respect toward others.

1. These behaviors will need to be modeled for the boys as many have learned to hide their deepest feelings. Role playing and creative dramatics will assist as will asking the basic question, "why?"

2. Provide activities where the boys can give supported positive comments to each other without embarrassment.

3. Show films and videotapes about showing respect and disrespect for others. List both types of activities on the board and discuss with the boys how alternate approaches may be used to correct disrespectable acts.

4. Have the boys role play both respectful and disrespectful acts.

5. Provide pictures showing both respectful and disrespectful acts. Discuss with the boys how they felt about each type of act.

6. Role play activities showing feelings and sympathy toward others.

7. Instruct the boys to develop stories showing feelings and sympathy toward others.

8. Use puppets to demonstrate and show feeling and respect toward others.

General Objective No. 4 of the Unit:
Young African-American males will use appropriate communication skills to develop new friendships and rekindle old ones.

Specific Objectives:
A. Review the importance of communication skills in developing appropriate interpersonal skills.
B. Develop activities and games to better acquaint the boys with each other.
C. Discuss the meaning of friendship. Outline ways that friendships may be developed.
D. Identify and articulate the characteristics of a good friend.
E. Provide the boys with the knowledge to distinguish between friendly and unfriendly actions.
F. Provide activities for the boys to address the group on several points of interest. Develop criteria to evaluate the topics.
G. Invite other classes to group activities such as talks and games; elicit their input.

Recommended Activities: (individualize and expand as needed)
A. Review the importance of communication skills in developing appropriate interpersonal skills. Communication is an important component in developing social skills. The following are suggestions for building a communicative environment for the classroom. When used at the beginning, these exercises can help the boys rekindle old friendships and develop new ones.

1. Review with the boys the relationship between communication skills and developing appropriate interpersonal skills.

2. Teach the boys how to properly express themselves in public places.

3. Provide activities to make the boy aware of appropriate language to use at public and social functions.

4. Model techniques for teaching the boys how to monitor their oral expression at social functions.

5. Have the boys critique each others' communication skills while demonstrating social and interpersonal skills.

6. Use high-profile individuals to compare their communication and interpersonal skills with those of the boys.

7. Provide many activities for the boys to express themselves.

B. Develop activities and games to better acquaint the boys with each other.

1. Instruct the boys how to play "people hunt." Have the boys move around the classroom in order to learn more about their classmates. Tell the boys to move about for five minutes to collect a different classmate's signature for each item on the list. The list could contain items such as the following:

a. has a bird for a pet
b. has black hair
c. has the shortest hair in the room
d. likes popcorn
e. has two brothers
f. has one sister
g. is the oldest child in the family
h. has been on a fishing trip
i. likes science best of all school subjects
j. was born in June
k. has won a medal in a sports competition

2. Group the boys by special characteristics such as birthdays. Have the boys indicate what day of the month they were born.

3. Provide activities for the boys to share their interests with the class. Classmates with similar interests may be invited to share their experiences.

4. Have the boys write stories about their favorite friends. Have the boys identify similar characteristics between them.

C. Discuss the meaning of friendship. Outline ways that friendships may be developed.

1. Divide students into teams of three or four and provide each boy with a form. Inform the boys that, as a team, they must decide on a list of characteristics

they all agree are important in a friend. Have them list three characteristics on the form.
2. Each team must work together to rank the characteristics on order of importance. Review with the boys that the characteristic they have agreed upon is the most important should be listed as number 1, number 2, and so on. Instruct the boys to complete the remainder of the form by themselves. Tell the boys to look over the form and decide which characteristics can best be applied to themselves.
3. Explain to the boys that sometimes when working in a group, positions or ideas have to be agreed upon so that the group can come to a decision. Have the boys share their experiences with the group process and determine whether they can come up with a group answer. If the boys have different answers, ask them to describe their answers to the large group.
4. Have the boys share their forms with the class.
5. Discuss with the boys what constitutes good friendship. What are the components of good friendship?
6. Summarize how friendships may be developed and maintained.
7. Develop the concept that it is "okay" for boys to develop friendships with girls.
D. Identify and articulate the characteristics of a good friend.
1. Discuss the characteristics of a good friend. Ask the boys to list at least five important friendship attributes, such as humor, availability, kindness, loyalty, and common interests.
2. Write characteristics that are suggested on the chalkboard. Refer to them again and add to them as the class thinks of new descriptions. Encourage the boys to write their own "recipes" for how to make a friend.
3. Have the boys work in teams to develop a mutually agreed-upon recipe. The team's final recipe can be written on an index card in a "recipe" format. A cookbook may be used as a guide.
4. Instruct the boys to draw pictures relevant to characteristics or attributes of good friendship.
5. Using pictures and photographs, have the boys identify attributes of a good friendship.
6. Have the boys write stories about how they met their best friends.

E. Provide the boys with the knowledge to distinguish between friendly and unfriendly actions.

    1. Make a circle and cut it out. Divide the circle into at least eight parts. Cut a dial hand/spinner using a piece of plastic. Attach the spinner to the center of the wheel with a paper fastener. Ask the boys to think of ways to be friendly. Write down appropriate deeds in each section of the circle. Provide opportunity for each boy to spin the wheel and discuss the deed where the pointer stopped.

    2. Cut out and glue small photographs that the boys have brought from home onto a piece of chart paper. Have the boys classify friendly and unfriendly behaviors from the photographs.

    3. Make a chart categorizing friendly and unfriendly behaviors; record input from the boys.

    4. Identify friendly and unfriendly behaviors from stories and pictures.

    5. Assist the boys in constructing stories about friendly and unfriendly behaviors.

    6. From the list of friendly and unfriendly actions in #3, have the boys give examples of the two types of behaviors.

F. Provide activities for the boys to address the group on several points of interests. Develop criteria for evaluating the topics.

    1. Discuss with the boys standards for evaluating reports. Include such factors as:

        a. Being polite to the speaker

        b. Showing respect for the speaker

        c. Not interrupting the speaker

        d. Saving questions to the end of the presentation

        e. Giving a valid criticism for a disagreement

    2. For boys who have similar interests, permit them to report in groups.

    3. Overview a common format for giving oral presentations. Instruct the boys that preparation is needed when giving reports.

    4. Invite the librarian to instruct the boys on library techniques and finding information on selected topics.

G. Invite other classes to group activities such as talks and games; elicit their input.

1. Expand the circle of friends by inviting other classes to participate.
2. Attempt to develop teams involving other boys from different classes.
3. New teams may report to joint classes. The format for evaluating reports in #1 is used.
4. A joint culminating activity involving all of the classes may be presented to the total school relevant to friendly and unfriendly actions.
5. Group art projects may be developed and posted throughout the school.

General Objective No. 5 of the Unit:
Young African-American males will acquire self-confidence and employ appropriate social skills at home, school, and the community.

Specific Objectives:
A. The boys will demonstrate how to cope with their feelings and emotions arising from conflicts.
B. The boys will practice acceptable social behaviors at school, home, and in the community.
C. The boys will accept praise when given.
D. The boys will accept criticism when given and demonstrate how to use the information for self-improvement.
E. The boys will develop a sense of pride and self-confidence.
F. The boys will control their anger when provoked.
G. The boys will understand the impact of their behavior upon others.

Recommended Activities: (individualize and expand as needed)
A. The boys will demonstrate how to cope with their feelings and emotions arising from conflicts.
1. From newspapers, films, filmstrips and tapes, show pictures of sad, happy, and angry faces. Have the boys explain how the people are feeling.
2. Have the boys draw faces showing a variety of expressions. Have the boys discuss and interpret their pictures, relating how the expressions can be changed.
3. Role play conditions that may create anger among the boys. Model and demonstrate ways of controlling anger.
4. Practice behavior intervention strategies with the boys to assist them in controlling anger. Praise the boys for successful attempts.

5. Provide activities where the boys can talk out their anger. Demonstrate how unacceptable behaviors are not appropriate ways for expressing anger. Model and demonstrate strategies.

B. The boys will practice acceptable behaviors at school, home, and in the community.

1. Discuss rules and laws with the boys. Explain that rules are made for our protection. Have the boys discuss classroom, home, and community rules.

2. When the boys break a rule, explain why obeying rules is important. Elicit responses from the boys about how rules protect us.

3. Role play situations. Show appropriate and inappropriate behaviors at school, home, and in the community. Have the boys critique each situation.

4. Show filmstrips, films, and videos of individuals displaying appropriate behavior.

5. Provide training for parents to use interpersonal skills to improve acceptable behaviors.

C. The boys will accept praise when given.

1. Develop activities such as demonstrations, role playing, modeling, and using magazines showing males accepting praise.

2. Discuss with the boys that accepting praise is not a sign of weakness, but strength; when praising, individuals are attempting to show appreciation of tasks well done.

3. Provide activities throughout the day where the boys are praised for successfully completing assigned tasks.

4. Role play activities where an authoritative male is accepting praise. Have the boys to discuss why.

D. The boys will accept criticism and use the information for self-improvement.

1. Role play situations in which the boys are criticized by each other. Demonstrate activities showing the boys how to respond to criticisms by explaining that the criticisms are not true.

2. When situations arise in which the boys behave badly, explain how their behaviors have affected the class. Require them to state an appropriate way that the situation could have been handled.

3. Discuss and model for the boys positive types of criticisms; compare with negative criticisms.

4. Show films and videotapes where criticisms are true; provide activities by which the boys will show how to use negative criticisms for self-improvement.

E. The boys will develop confidence in self by actively participating in group and individual activities.

1. Discuss the concept of a family; relate the concept of a family to the class. Provide activities where the boys have to work as a unit.

2. Assign the boys to teams of four or five, where each team will have a task to complete. Encourage each boy to do his share as a member of the team.

3. Encourage parents to include the boys in family activities. Give praise when earned as a contributing member of the group.

4. Provide activities where the boys must assume leadership. Their leadership will determine the success or the failure of the activity.

5. Provide the boys with situations in which they must make a decision. Give support, guidance, and praise until an appropriate decision is made.

F. The boys will control their anger when provoked.

1. Use puppets; have puppets call each other names. Discuss with the boys techniques for ignoring name calling.

2. Provide a system for rewarding and praising the boys when they ignore name calling.

3. Role play situations in which puppets call each other names because of an accidental bump or some other situation. Stress that name calling is unpleasant, but frequently it is best to ignore it.

4. Discuss with the boys that frequently name calling reflects insecurity on the part of the other person, and that the best way of dealing with the problem is to ignore it.

G. The boys will understand the impact of their behaviors upon others.

1. Videotape inappropriate behaviors of the boys. Discuss how these behaviors impacted others.

2. Have the boys discuss incidents where negative behaviors have affected them.

3. Role play situations where inappropriate or negative behaviors have caused others to be sad.

4. During activities in the classroom, encourage the boys to ask if an activity is disturbing to others. Remind the boys to be considerate of others.
5. Develop signals to indicate to the boys that their negative behaviors are affecting others.
6. On bulletin boards, have the boys draw pictures and narrate how positive behaviors impact others.
7. Encourage parents to implement and to follow up strategies at home.

General Objective No. 6 of the Unit:
Young African-American males will use social skills strategies to solve problems by communicating appropriately with others at home, community, and school.

Special Objectives:
A. The boys will practice the art of compromising.
B. The boys will demonstrate the need to anticipate sequences.
C. The boys will understand the need to set appropriate goals.
D. The boys will develop the skill of looking at alternatives.
E. The boys will know where to find good advice.
F. The boys will recognize emergency situations.
G. The boys will demonstrate how to interrupt appropriately.

Recommended Activities: (individualize and expand as needed)
A. The boys will practice the art of compromising.
1. Create situations that offer the boys a chance for compromise. Encourage the boys to practice the art of compromising. Provide guidance when needed.
2. Demonstrate and model compromises with the boys. Use different occasions and events to demonstrate compromising strategies.
3. Provide activities where the boys have to compromise. Provide guidance and praise to the boys for being cooperative and accepting the compromises.
4. Provide opportunities for the boys to make choices. When choices conflict, discuss the role of compromising.
B. The boys will demonstrate the need to anticipate consequences.
1. Role play situations in which the consequences of behaviors are anticipated by the boys.
2. As the boys participate in instructional activities, encourage them to anticipate the consequences of their behaviors.

3. Read the boys stories, show filmstrips, and have them anticipate the consequences of the characters' behaviors.

4. Provide activities that require the boys to think through behaviors by considering the consequences before reacting.

C. The boys will understand the need to set appropriate goals.

1. Provide time to discuss with the boys the importance of setting realistic goals.

2. Assign activities that will aid the boys in achieving their goals.

3. Initiate and review a variety of techniques to enable the boys to self-monitor their achievements toward accomplishing their goals.

4. Provide support and encouragement to the boys; praise them frequently.

5. Review films, stories, and videotapes about famous individuals. Have the boys discuss whether or not they thought that these individuals have well-defined goals.

D. The boys will develop the skill of looking at alternatives.

1. Plan activities where the boys are introduced to alternative ways of solving problems.

2. Encourage the boys to "try another way" when their initial approaches do not appear to be working. Provide demonstrations and models for the boys to imitate. Give praise frequently.

3. Role play several situations using alternative approaches to conflict resolutions.

E. The boys will know where to find good advice.

1. Visit community agencies, such as recreational centers, health clubs, and public libraries. Discuss the purposes and roles of these organizations, pointing out specific services they provide.

2. Invite community individuals to talk with the boys on selected topics. Develop a pool of volunteers to be available for the boys to consult.

3. Role play situations in which the boys are seeking both good and bad advice. Include situations the boys are likely to experience.

4. Place pictures of community helpers on a bulletin board with a description of their duties. Review situations in which the boys may appropriately react with them.

F. The boys will recognize emergency situations.

1. Discuss with the boys how to avoid emergency situations such as name calling, fighting, stealing, and other aggressive acts. Model and role play several situations.

2. During instructional activities, remind the boys not to interrupt. Praise them for successful attempts.

3. Develop strategies that give the boys clues concerning their time to talk, such as if someone asks a question or stops talking.

4. Role play situations in which the boys are introduced to each other. Encourage them to respond to each other appropriately, to take turns speaking, and not to interrupt each other. Praise the boys for their efforts.

General Objective No. 7 of the Unit:
Young African-American males will demonstrate how to experience positive self-acceptance and awareness.

Specific Objectives:
A. The boys will recognize that changing old habits is very difficult and requires a systematic plan.

B. The boys will identify individuals who can assist them in bringing about positive changes.

C. Have the boys provide a monitoring and follow-up plan to assist them in making changes.

D. Have the boys accent the positive things that they do in the class; have them to praise each other frequently.

E. Have the boys discuss special traits and characteristics of each other.

Recommended Activities: (individualize and expand as needed)
A. Instruct the boys that changing old habits are very difficult and requires a systematic plan.

1. Assist the boys in identifying the source of the problems. Make sure they are able to briefly describe the problem and explain why they consider it to be a problem.

2. Instruct students to brainstorm as many solutions to the problem as they can. A good practice is for the student to write all the possibilities down.

3. Have students now look through the possibilities and choose two or three "best" choices.

4. Have the boys discuss how they might arrive at the solution to the problem. Have each boy list the solutions.

5. Develop group activities whereby the group chooses the solution that appears to be the best.

6. Guide the boys in constructing a course of action for changing old negative habits.

7. Monitor the plan frequently with feedback to the boys.

B. Identify individuals who can assist the boys in bringing about positive changes.

1. Direct the boys to list individuals whom they trust. Have them indicate why they trust these individuals.

2. Expand the discussions by having the boys indicate how selected individuals may help them change negative habits.

3. Review film and videotapes showing famous Black individuals. Ask the boys questions such as:

a. What do you like about the individual?

b. How do you believe these individuals can contribute to bringing about positive change?

c. Do you know anything about the history of this individual?

4. Using the dialogue established in #3, choose two or three famous Black individuals and summarize their histories.   Point out how they overcame adverse conditions as well as individuals who assisted them in bringing about positive changes.

5. Discuss with the boys what might have happened if these Black individuals had not changed some of their negative behaviors.

6. Role play some of the famous Blacks; emphasize how they brought about positive changes.

7. Have the boy develop stories about Blacks who overcame adverse conditions.

C. Provide a monitoring and follow-up plan to assist the boys in making changes.

1. Develop an evaluation sheet for each boy. Boys indicate daily on the chart progress made toward making changes in their behaviors. (See Appendix E for an example of an evaluation sheet).

2. Check the evaluation sheet weekly and confer individually with each boy, highlighting "positives" and minimizing "negatives".

3. Develop a system for rewarding the boys for keeping their evaluation sheets in order as well as showing improvement.

4. Teach the boys how to graph their progress for the week by showing the number for each category. Assist them in interpreting what the graphs show.

5. Use role models in the school and community to demonstrate how successful changes can be made.

6. Have a talk show where the boys can relate how they brought about changes.

7. Discuss with the boys factors that should be considered when planning changes.

D. Accent the positive things that the boys do in the class; praise frequently.

1. Frequently use positive statements about good deeds.

2. Provide opportunities for the boys to discover positive things about themselves through role playing and creative dramatics.

3. Develop a Citizen of the Week Award; stipulate the criteria or standards for achieving the award.

4. Develop activities where all boys can be successful and award them for achieving the success.

5. Have something positive to say about each boy each day.

6. Use boys as models to assist in shaping positive behaviors.

E. Discuss special traits and characteristics of the boys. Provide opportunities for each boy to record his special traits.

1. Through observations and interviews with the boys and parents, determine special traits and abilities of each boy.

2. Use the knowledge gained from #1 to develop specific activities for the boys to complete. Motivation and success should be high because of the high interest rate.

3. Catch the boys being good and videotape their behaviors with permission from parents. Show and discuss behaviors with the class.

4. Associate videotapes of positive behaviors with classroom rules and acts of courtesy.

5. Photograph both negative and positive behaviors with permission from parents. Post photographs on the board under appropriate behaviors or inappropriate behaviors. Discuss ways in which inappropriate behaviors can be made appropriate.

6. Using information from the bulletin board, have the boys role play both types of behaviors.

7. Determine special abilities of the boys as outlined in #1, and assign them special functions, such as setting up and operating the film projector.

EVALUATION OF SOCIAL SKILLS

General evaluation techniques were outlined in Chapter 4. If evaluation results are to be effectively used to gauge to what extent the stated objectives have been achieved, the evaluation process must be properly planned. First, a decision must be made on what to evaluate. This approach facilitates the selection of appropriate methods and techniques such as:

1. Evaluating the competence of a particular social skill.

2. Determining the baseline behavior for a particular social skill.

3. Using results to revise the curriculum.

4. Providing information to gauge the progress of the boys.

5. Appraising the effectiveness of selected social skills activities.

6. Making sure that the boys demonstrate the necessary prerequisites/skills for performing the social skills.

7. Having the necessary physical and human resources to conduct the unit.

8. Eliciting the cooperation of parents.

9. Providing training for parents to follow up social skills at home.

10. Determining the reactions of the boys toward selected activities.

INFORMAL EVALUATION TECHNIQUES

Techniques for evaluating the social skills development of young African-American males come in many forms, including formal and informal techniques. Chapter 4 outlined formal techniques. This section will address informal procedures. These techniques are readily accessible or can easily be developed by the classroom teacher. Some recommended strategies include:

1. Develop a brief checklist to assess social skills in a variety of situations.

2. Simulate social activities requiring the boys to portray different roles that can be used to assess their understanding of appropriate behaviors in various settings. Group and individual appraisal of the activity may be conducted by the class.

3. Use group assignments to evaluate the boys' ability to work cooperatively. Record specific incidents, appropriate and inappropriate.

4. Model and provide illustrations of appropriate and inappropriate behaviors. Have the boys demonstrate both types of behaviors and discriminate between them.

5. Structure activities and situations that call for specific kinds of behaviors and observe the performance of the boys. A rating scale may be used.

6. Assess the frequency of inappropriate behaviors; assist the boys in monitoring their own behaviors.

7. With parental permission, use a variety of audio-visual aids such as films and filmstrips depicting appropriate and inappropriate social skills. Have the boys critique what is taking place and give alternative responses.

Sample Evaluation Checklist for Evaluating Social Skills Demonstrated Social Skills Competence

General Objective	Specific Objectives	Pre- Yes No	Post- Yes No
I. Young African-American males will achieve socially acceptable behaviors in social and inter-personal situations.	a. The boys will respect members of the opposite sex.	___ ___	___ ___
	b. The boys will demonstrate appropriate character traits needed for acceptance in the public.	___ ___	___ ___
	c. The boys will show respect for the rights and properties of others.	___ ___	___ ___

d. The boys will recognize authority and follow instructions of school, home, and the community.   __ __ __ __

e. The boys will recognize personal roles in public places.   __ __ __ __

II. Young African-American males will acquire self-confidence and employ appropriate social skills at home, school, and community.

a. The boys will demonstrate how to cope with their feelings and emotions arising from conflicts.   __ __ __ __

b. The boys will practice acceptable social behaviors at home, school, and community.   __ __ __ __

c. The boys will accept praise when given.   __ __ __ __

d. The boys will accept criticism when given and demonstrate how to use the information for self-improvement.   __ __ __ __

e. The boys will develop a sense of pride and self-confidence in themselves.   __ __ __ __

III. Young African-American males will use social skills strategies to solve problems by communicating appropriately to others at school, home, and community.

a. The boys will practice the art of compromising.   __ __ __ __

b. The boys will demonstrate the need to anticipate consequences.   __ __ __ __

c. The boys will demonstrate the need to set appropriate goals.   __ __ __ __

d. The boys will develop the skill of looking at alternatives.   __ __ __ __

e. The boys will know where to find good advice.   __ __ __ __

f. The boys will recognize emergency situations.   __ __ __ __

g. The boys will demonstrate how to interrupt appropriately.   __ __ __ __

Informal evaluation results, such as the Checklist, may be used to determine if social intervention is needed as well as grouping boys into different instructional groups to remediate the social deficits.

Activities and creative games can be designed to improve social greetings, developing good relationships, respecting the feelings of others, practicing common courtesy, ways to make friends, acceptable ways to show anger, alternatives to cursing, learning when an apology is needed, appropriate and inappropriate touching, being a good sport, and the importance of being a good neighbor. Activities should be age-appropriate. Specific objectives are stated for each area of social skills development, with specific directions and procedures for completing each activity followed by a list of specific questions for children. Desired outcomes are also listed for each activity. an assessment sheet is provided to evaluate social growth. Games and activities may be infused into the curriculum, or common criteria may be developed by the teacher with specific conditions for playing the games. Games and activities may be placed in a learning center or station.

Social skills should not be taught in isolation, but infused throughout the curriculum as needed. Approach and strategies outlined are not meant to be exclusive. Adaptations and modifications are encouraged.

The strategies and interventions reported have been tested with young African-American males and found to be successful. Results have shown a decrease in negative behaviors and an increase in positive behaviors and achievement. Specific techniques for evaluating the impact of social skills in reducing inappropriate behaviors were comprehensively outlined in Chapter 4.

It is recommended that this type of checklist be revised for all of the social skills taught. The checklist or other informal techniques should be administered on a pre/posttest basis. Such a procedure permits the teacher to objectively determine to what degree the stated objectives have been achieved and to determine modifications or adaptations needed in the unit.

SUMMARY

In social skills training, young African-American males are taught those skills they must master if they are to become contributing members of society. Emphasis has been placed on developing instructional activities that assist these boys in functioning successfully at school, home, and the community in social situations. Activities have been developed that help the boys control their tempers, initiate compromises, and develop improved interpersonal relationships and strategies for recognizing and respecting authority.

An excellent resource book to promote social skills is Social Skills: Learning to Get Along with Other People[1].

NOTE

1. Haugen, J. (1993). *Learning to get along with other people.* San Antonio, TX: PCI Publishing Co.

9

Summary

It is commonly thought that young children react to social conflict using different standards than adults. DiMartino's (1990) study refuted this myth, however. His study showed that areas of social conflict in this experiment included: (1) morality, (2) social convention, (3) safety, and (4) institutional rules.

The same premise may be applied to young African-American males, since all children basically precede through the same social developmental stages; however, some young African-American males appear to be at the highest risk for social development. Studies have shown that at-risk young African-American males attained the lowest average on academic achievement scores and were over-represented in categories such as retained students, school drop-outs, suspended and expelled students, and referral to special education. These findings confirm that young African-American males are at risk during the early elementary grades.

A significant number of young African-American males are educated in public schools located in urban communities, many of which do not provide good environments in which to educate these boys. Thus, a multitude of problems work against the boys receiving appropriate education. (1) The average young African-American male at risk lives with a single parent whose income is below or at the poverty level. This parent is frequently female. (2) Many young African-American males are exposed daily to violence and physical and drug abuse. (3) Many of the boys receive inadequate nutrition and health care. Combined, these factors contribute to many mental, social, and physical problems that impede successful academic and social development.

Holland (1989) summed up the plight of young African-American males by stating that drastic reforms must be made in urban education.

Specifically, strategies and interventions must be focused on the individual needs of Black males in the primary grades and must be integrated and coordinated with available community resources.

Many African-American males have developed or adopted alternative ways and styles of coping with problems in their neighborhoods. These behavioral styles are frequently in conflict with the standards of schools and society in general, and may be viewed as negative or destructive. Thus, behavioral styles and models copied and imitated by young African-American males may serve them well in their environments, but are frequently viewed as dysfunctional by the school and society.

Many young African-American males tend to settle differences by physical means. This approach may be attributed to poor impulse control. Also, frequently, they do not accept responsibility for their actions but attribute blame to others for negative and inappropriate behaviors. Generally, young African-American males who are at risk, tend to demonstrate lower interpersonal skills compared with other children. It is believed that poor interpersonal skills can be directly attributed to the lack of social skills training during the developmental years.

The value of social skills training for young African-American males has been well documented throughout this text. Social skills training should be considered as an ongoing intervention strategy. Opportunities should be provided in the curriculum for the boys to internalize appropriate behaviors as they develop additional ways of interacting with others. Instructional programs must be developed and designed to enable young African-American males to gain knowledge about appropriate interpersonal skills and to employ this newly acquired knowledge in solving their social problems. In order for this goal to be accomplished, young African-American males must be taught effective ways of internalizing their behaviors and assessing how their behaviors affect others.

Teaching appropriate social skills to young African-American males appears to be a promising technique for improving pro-social skills (Taylor, 1992). For example, appropriate social skills are essential for developing personal relationships and accepting the roles of authority figures. Social behaviors are learned; therefore, they can be changed and modified. Proper social skills require that an individual evaluate a situation, choose the appropriate social skills, and perform the social tasks accordingly (Katz, 1991). Unfortunately, many young African-American males have not been exposed to appropriate social models or do not possess enough prerequisite skills, such as maturity and self-control, to successfully perform the social skills (Taylor, 1992).

Research findings have clearly demonstrated that diverse groups of children, including young African-American males, are at risk for developing appropriate interpersonal skills. Lack of such skills may lead to feelings of rejection and isolation in classroom settings. There is also ample evidence to suggest that children's social difficulties may emanate from different sources and areas. These deficit areas must be identified and remediated during the early years. Schools must design direct and implement intervention programs that permit these young African-American males to experience success (Butler, 1988; Hilliard, 1989; Kagan, 1989; Bradley, et al., 1989; Diggory, 1990; Foster, 1986; Deal, 1990; Holland, 1987; Ayers, 1989).

Studies have consistently shown that negative behaviors are learned behaviors that children imitate from their environments. Frequently, these hostile and destructive patterns of behavior cannot be controlled by the schools, thus creating conflict and tension between children, parents, and school (Matsueda & Heimer, 1987; Gibbs, 1988).

The preponderance of studies in the area of social learning have consistently shown that the learning styles of some young African-American males are significantly different from those of their peers. Society and the school have failed to capitalize on this salient point. The school has not changed its basic approach to teaching these children over the last several decades, in spite of the vast amount of research and literature on innovative teaching techniques and strategies.

School experiences for young African-American males are usually unrelated to the experiences they bring to school. Their abilities to function satisfactorily in social groups are usually below expected levels set by the school. They have fewer and less rigid control over their impulses and have learned hostile and destructive patterns of behavior as viewed by society and the school. The majority of young African-American males at risk will never become fully integrated in society and the school unless early intervention is attempted and social skills are infused and systematically taught throughout the curriculum. It is incumbent upon the school to recognize and accept this fact and to develop strategies to modify, adapt, and gradually promote what is considered to be "appropriate social behavior" through the use of behavior intervention techniques and other strategies.

Personality, temperament, cognitive styles, sociological influences, and ethnic background may all influence the development and learning of young African-American males. The study of social learning theories enables the school to understand both how these boys' cultures can be modified to promote expected learning outcomes and how these boys feel about themselves in relationship to learning. Social skills activities and strategies must be developed to promote the emotional well-being of young African-American males. This approach appears to be in concert with one of the basic premises of this book, which is that a school system that does not deem the teaching of interpersonal skills as important as academic skills may not be preparing its youth for successful democratic participation in our society.

Some observations that appear relevant to educating at risk young African-American males and creating effective interpersonal learning strategies include:

1. Seem generally unaware of the "ground rules" for success in school.
2. Are less able to learn from being told than are their counterparts.
3. Are often unable to make simple symbolic interpretations.
4. Tend to have shorter attention spans and consequently have problems in following directions.
5. Are unable to use language in a flexible way.
6. Tend to have little concept of relative size of objects outside their environments.
7. Are less likely to perceive adults as people to whom they can turn to for help.
8. Seem to have a low level of curiosity about things.
9. Seem to project a low self-image.
10. Have experiences within a very narrow range.

The difficult part of teaching is not developing appropriate learning strategies for young African-American males, but dealing with the great influx of children who come from emotionally, physically, socially, and financially stressed homes. This is not a school problem alone; society in general must assume the major responsibilities for these environmental atrocities. The school is responsible to the extent that is has not used the vast amount of research and resources to change teaching techniques to educate many young African-American males. For these children, school experiences have virtually remained unchanged for decades. Additionally, teaching techniques are usually unrelated to the experiences they bring to school and do not adequately address the observations outlined. Life in school is mostly teacher-centered, textbook-dominated, restrictive, impersonal, and rigid (Goodland, 1984). Bridges (1988) summed up the status of education for at risk African-American males by stating that some models for Black male children's development are broken, and we must find solutions to fix them.

These issues and more must be addressed by the school if it is to become responsive to the educational needs of many young African-American males. Policies must be changed at the local, state, and national levels. The Committee for Economic Development (1987) advanced the position that our commitment to the young must go beyond political rhetoric and must produce a well planned curriculum of programs for children from birth through adulthood. This appears to be appropriate for schools to promote in providing equal education opportunities for all children, including young African-American males.

Appendix A: Instructional and Intervention Strategies for Instructing Young African-American Males

List of Recommended Social Skills To Be Taught
Components of Male Class

I. Bonding
    A. Pledge (first thing in the morning)
    B. Acknowledgment of Unity
        1. Handshake; secret signal; cue; smile.
        2. Words "we are family."
    C. Buddy (Explain to students:)
        1. A buddy can be selected for each unit to work with in the completion of a long-range project.
        2. A buddy you can work with in co-operative learning groups.
        3. A buddy you can share a common interest with (give an interest survey).
        4. A buddy you may eat lunch with, telephone to check over homework with, share a book with, walk with in line.

II. Social Skills
    A. Basic Needs
        1. *Attention*—Allow children to take turns being group leaders, readers, student of the day.
        2. *Belonging*—Given name for the class, special pledge, motto, colors, other symbols that represent belonging.
        3. *Importance*—We need you today to help us with this task. Your team buddy needs you; your participation is valuable to the group; we are depending on your help. This is your assigned responsibility everyday. Without you, this doesn't operate smoothly. [Biography Board].
        4. *Confidence*—Praise; encouragement; present a task that seems to be complex but encourages the student toward mastery.
        5. *Sense of Freedom*—(Choices—point out to students:) Even in disciplinary situations; you can either do it now or after school. The choice is yours.

Fighting: how could you have handled him/her differently? What can I do to help with the problem? What do you feel you would like or need to do now?

B. Goals (Instruction should be used to foster:)
- Confidence
- Motivation
- Effort
- Responsibility
- Initiative
- Perseverance
- Caring
- Teamwork
- Common sense
- Problem-solving skills

III. Curriculum

A. African American Basis
- Infuse topics from Black History Unit
- Use alternative unit approach for social skills development

B. Suggested Topics:
- Ancient African kingdoms
- African myths and folklore
- The journey to America
- African/Egyptian math principals
- Slavery
- Famous scientists
- Famous sportsmen
- Famous inventors
- Famous educators
- Famous writers
- Famous entertainers

C. Integrate the buddy system, social skills, oral responses, values and writing, and research organization skills around units.

D. Suggested Other Units
- Animals
- Jobs
- Weather
- Mysterious phenomena
- Living things
- Food

E. Projects
- Drawings
- Posters
- Paper mache

---

* Males tend to solve conflicts on the spot, whereas females tend to harbor hostility and plot or plan to retaliate later.

Appendix B: Social Skills To Be Taught

INFORMAL ASSESSMENT INVENTORY

Directions: Check always, sometimes, or never for each statement. There are no correct or incorrect answers.

AGGRESSION	ALWAYS	SOMETIMES	NEVER
I get mad often.	_____	_____	_____
I find other children are friendly to me.	_____	_____	_____
I get angry when treated unfairly.	_____	_____	_____
People are always trying to get me.	_____	_____	_____
I usually hit first.	_____	_____	_____
I must always protect myself.	_____	_____	_____
I feel protected.	_____	_____	_____
I don't get upset if I see something torn or messed up.	_____	_____	_____
I like fixing broken things.	_____	_____	_____
People don't hear me unless I talk loud.	_____	_____	_____
I like to talk loud.	_____	_____	_____

ORGANIZATION

	ALWAYS	SOMETIMES	NEVER
I am no good at getting work done.	_____	_____	_____
I complete tasks easily.	_____	_____	_____
I remember my books and materials needed for that day.	_____	_____	_____
I have often lost my lunch ticket.	_____	_____	_____
I have never lost anything.	_____	_____	_____
I hang up my coat and put my books away when I arrive home.	_____	_____	_____
I copy my assignments down and turn them in on time.	_____	_____	_____

	ALWAYS	SOMETIMES	NEVER
I have trouble finding things in my room.	_____	_____	_____
It takes time to find papers asked for in my notebook.	_____	_____	_____
I have trouble trying to memorize facts and things.	_____	_____	_____
I remember the words to songs easily.	_____	_____	_____
I am doing well in school.	_____	_____	_____

BEHAVIOR PROBLEMS

	ALWAYS	SOMETIMES	NEVER
I get in trouble for many little things.	_____	_____	_____
Nobody pays any attention to me.	_____	_____	_____
I can be happy one minute and sad the next.	_____	_____	_____
When I see something I need, I ask for it.	_____	_____	_____
When I see something I need, I take it.	_____	_____	_____
Other people get me into trouble.	_____	_____	_____
I control my own actions.	_____	_____	_____
I need adults to tell me how to act.	_____	_____	_____

STRESS

	ALWAYS	SOMETIMES	NEVER
Sometimes, I feel like running away.	_____	_____	_____
I don't like to laugh.	_____	_____	_____
It's bad to make a mistake.	_____	_____	_____
It's better to keep your feelings to yourself.	_____	_____	_____
I like to take risks to grow and learn.	_____	_____	_____

	ALWAYS	SOMETIMES	NEVER
It is important for me to be the first in everything.	_____	_____	_____
I like to win at everything.	_____	_____	_____
I don't like for people to touch me or stand too close to me.	_____	_____	_____
I hate to wait for things.	_____	_____	_____
I get embarrassed easily.	_____	_____	_____

Appendix C: Observation Checklist

Observation Checklist

Teacher_____ Observer_____

Lesson_____ Date_____ Time_____

	NEVER	FREQUENTLY	ALWAYS
Student deals positively with accusations.	_____	_____	_____
Student accepts feelings of others in a nonthreatening manner.	_____	_____	_____
Student respects the feelings of others.	_____	_____	_____
Student knows how to avoid fights and conflicts and display good humor.	_____	_____	_____
Student deals effectively with teasing.	_____	_____	_____
Student moves about room independently to perform routine tasks.	_____	_____	_____
Student stays away from troublesome situations. Accepts culture values of pupils.	_____	_____	_____
Student verbally shows appreciation when assisted.	_____	_____	_____
Student gives praise or compliments to other students.	_____	_____	_____
Student accepts compliments from others.	_____	_____	_____
Student apologizes for inappropriate behavior.	_____	_____	_____
Student expresses anger in a positive way.	_____	_____	_____
Student attempts to understand another's anger without getting angry.	_____	_____	_____
Student shows affection and appreciation toward others.	_____	_____	_____

	NEVER	**FREQUENTLY**	**ALWAYS**
Student asks permission to borrow or use others' belongings.	_____	_____	_____
Student readily shares objects with others.	_____	_____	_____
Student practices self-control.	_____	_____	_____
Student disagrees in an acceptable manner.	_____	_____	_____
Student accepts losing without becoming upset.	_____	_____	_____
Student does not lose control when left out of group activities.	_____	_____	_____

Appendix D: Cooperative Learning Strategies

SOME COOPERATIVE LEARNING STRATEGIES
CIRCLE ACTIVITIES

Circle activities have been specifically designed to include many different groupings:

Full—The full circle implies that all students would participate in the circle topic and sit together in one circle.

Team—The approach is based on Slavin and Johnson's concepts of cooperative learning (Slavin, 1991; Johnson et al., 1988). Teams consist of five to six students representing different characteristics and abilities. Permanent team assignments are recommended in order to save time assigning teams for each activity.

Recommended strategies for forming cooperative teams include:

Select a name—Team members select a name, take a vote, and then introduce the name to the larger group.

Construct a logo—Members approve of the logo, which will be used to identify the team. The art teacher may be used as a resource if needed.

Develop a group profile—Provide each team with paper and supplies for designing a group profile on the paper showing each separate individual's interests/strengths /desires onto a team profile chart.

Partner—Provide activities for two students to work together. Students may choose their own partner. After a while, ask students to choose another student whom they do not know as well.

Cooperative Learning Tools

Many of the materials used in circle activities are already accessible in the classroom. Teachers are encouraged to be as creative and innovative as possible.

Puppets—Any puppet that is friendly looking is sufficient. The puppet introduces the circle activities and facilitates the discussion. Students may choose a puppet name or use the name of one of their story characters.

Timer—This can greatly facilitate circle discussions because it lets students know when the circle time is up. Set the timer for the designated time and inform students that when the timer buzzes, the circle is over.

Suggestion box—A small box with a removable top will suffice. Cut a slit $\frac{1}{2}$" × 5" along the top of the box. Have the children decorate the box and write "Suggestions" on the side in big bold letters. Students should be instructed to place their suggestions inside the box. Their suggestions may provide additional circle topics to discuss.

Name cards—Make a set of name cards on 3" × 5" strips of paper. Color code the cards using two colors. Divide the class in half; give the boys alternate colors. Colors may be changed as special events and holidays occur.

Writing book—Make a writing book ditto. Provide space for each student's name in the group. Make several copies of the sheet and staple them between construction paper covers. Use the book during circle time to record students' comments. On selected circles, name the topic at the top of the form and then quickly jot down the main idea of each student's contribution. This is also an incentive for listening.

Recommendations for increasing participation within groups and circles include:

1. **Accent strengths and uniqueness throughout the day.** Students won't be able to verbalize their strengths unless they are made aware of them.

2. **Have students keep individual records of their positive self-statements.**

3. **Model positive self-statements.** If students hear the teacher saying positive comments periodically about themselves, they'll begin to feel it's safe to do so too.

4. **Praise and support students for their use of positive self-statements.** Attempt to create an environment that's secure for such growth.

5. **Be supportive of any student who cannot quickly verbalize a positive self-statement in the circle.** Use whatever statement is generated and make a positive remark about it; seek approval and endorsement from the student.

6. **Discuss real-life experiences of students in the beginning circles.** Students are often more comfortable about sharing things that they have experienced. Invite students to bring something from home of which they are proud or have an interest in.

7. **Invite students to draw a picture of what they will be saying for the circle.** This is particularly helpful for shy students. The picture will provide support for the student during discussions.

Appendix E: Sample Evaluation Sheet

EVALUATION SHEET (Sample items may be expanded as needed)

	YES	NO	SOME-TIMES
I followed classroom and school rules today.	_____	_____	_____
I showed respect for others today.	_____	_____	_____
I attempted to control my anger today.	_____	_____	_____
Did I contribute to my group's discussions today?	_____	_____	_____
Did I practice good citizenship habits today?	_____	_____	_____
Was I on my best behavior today?	_____	_____	_____
Was I polite and courteous to my classmates today?	_____	_____	_____
Was I considerate of others today?	_____	_____	_____
Did I use negotiation strategies today?	_____	_____	_____
Did I consider the feelings of others before I responded.	_____	_____	_____
Did I show appreciation for a kind deed today?	_____	_____	_____
I added to my circle of friends today.	_____	_____	_____
I praised classmates for successful tasks completed today.	_____	_____	_____
I recorded my behavior on my performance chart today.	_____	_____	_____

Appendix F: Selected Resources

FILMS AND FILMSTRIPS

Aesop's Fables.   Nine color-captioned filmstrips.   Educational Projections Corporation. Titles: *The Mean Old Elephant, The Lion and the Goat, The Silly Rabbit, Wolf in Sheep's Clothing, The Loud-Mouthed Frog, The Greedy Dog, The Evil Spider, The Mouse Who Boasted,* and *The Foolish Donkey.* (1-3)

Animal Stories Series.   Six color filmstrips.   Educational Reading Service. These filmstrips are made up of photographs of children and their pets and teach responsibility and consideration of others.

Appreciating Our Parents. Color or black/white 16mm film. Coronet Films. This film is Aesop's fable "one good turn deserves another."

Beginning Responsibility: Being a Good Sport. Color or black/white 16mm film. Coronet Films. Poor sportsmanship over a checkers game leads to a discussion of sportsmanship.

Beginning Responsibility: Learning to Follow Directions. One reel; color or black/white. Coronet. Some of David's toy animals magically come to life and teach him that he must pay attention.

Beginning Responsibility: Lunchroom Manners. Color or black/white 16mm film. Coronet Films. Through a puppet show, the children in a class realize that clumsiness and impoliteness are funny with Mr. Bungle, but are not desirable among themselves. (1-3)

But It Isn't Yours. Two filmstrips, one 12-inch LP record or cassette, and teacher's guide. Guidance Associates. Two unfinished stories included are these: Part 1, Is it permissible for Bill to keep a dog which has escaped from the pound?, Part 2, Is Jeff responsible for returning stolen property that he unknowingly accepted? (K-4)

Conduct and Behavior. Ten color-captioned filmstrips. Educational Projections Corporation. Titles: *In School, On the Playground, On the Street, At Home, Visiting Friends, Traveling, Shopping, In Public Buildings, The Picnic,* and *Responsibility.*

Developing Basic Values.   Four color filmstrips and records or cassettes and teacher's guides. Society for Visual Education, Incorporated. Titles: *Respect for Property, Consideration of Others, Acceptance of Others,* and *Recognition of Responsibilities.*

Fairness for Beginners. Color or black/white 16mm film. Coronet Films. The film presents the ways of being fair: sharing, taking turns, choosing fairly, and respecting the rights of others.

Getting To Know Me. Four color filmstrips with two records or cassettes and teacher's guide. Society for Visual Education. The film is designed to develop self-understanding and self-acceptance. Titles: *People Are Like Rainbows, A Boat Named George, Listen! Jimmy!,* and *Strike Three! You're In.*

Good Citizens. Encyclopedia Britannica Educational Corporation, 1961. The file discusses courtesy, cooperation, dependability, and fair play.

Good Manners. Series of six filmstrips (average 48 frames each). Encyclopedia Britannica Educational Corporation. Good manners are presented as a means of getting along with people.

Guidance Stories, Series No.8490. Six color filmstrips. Encyclopedia Britannica Educational Corporation Titles: *Sharing With Others, Playing Fair, Sticking to Your Job, New Friends - Good Friends, One Kind of Bravery,* and *Taking Care of Your Things.*

Late for Dinner: Was Dawn Right? Color or black/white 16mm film. Encyclopedia Britannica Educational Corporation. An open-ended film shows that conflicting feelings are normal.

Little Citizen Series. Society for Visual Education, 1960. The film highlights students' responsibility toward others.

Little Things That Count. Eight color filmstrips with four records or cassette Teach-A-Tapes and teacher's manual. Eye Gate House. Freedom's Foundation Awards Winner. The stories involve the joy of helping others, honesty, perseverance, responsibility, justice, reverence, and love.

Minorities and Majorities. Six color filmstrips with three cassette Teach-A-Tapes and teacher's manual. Eye Gate House. The film deals with child-to-child prejudice, being part of a group, being outside of the group, and being within a group. Ethnic, national, religious, and color distinctions are not discussed as issues.

Practicing Good Citizenship. Six filmstrips; individual filmstrips also available. Troll Associates, 1972. Film titles: *Growing Up To Be A*

Good Citizen; When To Be A Leader, When To Be A Follower; Recognizing Individual Differences; A Good Citizen In School; Be A Danger Fighter; and A Newcomer Comes To Town.

Tales of the Wise Old Owl. Filmstrips and records in three groups. Society for Visual Education. Group 1: *Dr. Retriever's Surprise and Silly Excuses.* Group 2: *Bushy the Squirrel and Peggy the Pup.* Group 3: *The Feather That Was Lost* and *Pearl of Great Price.*

Teaching Children Values Through Unfinished Stories. Two color filmstrips, one 33 1/3 rpm record or cassette, and teacher's guide. Educational Activities, Inc. Open-ended stories enable the pupil to identify with the central character and to think about and devise solutions to problems offered.

That's Not Fair. Two filmstrips with record or cassette. Guidance Associates. Part 1: Is it fair to take another's place in a gift line? Part 2: Two boys return some lost spectacles and are undecided about how to share the reward, which is a watch.

The Ant and The Dove. Color or black/white 16mm film. Coronet Films. This film is Aesop's fable, "One good turn deserves another."

The "Be Kind" Stories. Four color filmstrips with two cassette Teach-A-Tapes and teacher's manual; coloring books available. Eye Gate House. The emphasis is on expressing more kindness in everyday living.

The Lemonade Stand: What's Fair? Color or black/white 16mm film. Encyclopedia Britannica Educational Corporation. Focuses on the meaning of commitment, obligations, and responsibility to others.

The Picture Life of Thurgood Marshall. Young, M.B. Watts, 1971. A brief biography of the Black lawyer who fights for the rights of African-American citizens and eventually becomes the first Black man to become an Associate Justice of the Supreme Court.

The Report Card: How Does Ricardo Feel? Color or black/white 16mm film. Encyclopedia Britannica Educational Corporation. The film teaches that when individuals do not control their emotions, anger can be destructive.

Values. Six color filmstrips with three cassette Teach-A-Tapes or filmstrips with cassettes. Eye Gate House, 1972. Film titles: *Telling the Truth, What Is Stealing?, Kindness, Politeness, Responsibility,* and *Citizenship.* This film is designed to help the student develop a standard of values; both appropriate and inappropriate responses to a conflict situation are given without a judgement being made. By discussing or role playing each problem and response, students can develop their own answers and formulate their own set of values.

Ways To Settle Disputes. One reel; color or black/white. Collaborator: Carter Davidson. The film emphasizes that settlement of conflict must be desired to be effective and gives four ways of settling disputes.

What Do You Expect Of Others? Three filmstrips, one 12-inch LP record or cassette, and teacher's guide. Guidance Associates. The film helps children learn that what you expect a person to be like has much to do with how he or she acts toward you.

What Happens Between People? Two filmstrips, one 12-inch LP record or cassette, and teacher's guide. Guidance Associates. The film assists children in becoming aware of types of human interactions between individuals and groups.

You Got Mad: Are You Glad? Two filmstrips, one 12-inch LP record or cassette, and teacher's guide. Guidance Associates. The film helps children discover the cause and effects of hostility, stressing behavioral choices such as mediation, third-party judgment, and compromise as ways to resolve conflicts.

Yours, Mine, and Ours. Color or black/white 16mm film. Encyclopedia Britannica Educational Corporation. Reflects classroom situations showing proper responsibility for ownership; teacher children to recognize group and individual responsibilities.

RECORDS

Aesop's Fables. 12-inch LP record. Caedman (Alesco). Boris Karloff reads 42 classic moral and ethical tales. (1-6)

American Poems of Patriotism. 12-inch LP record. Caedman (Alesco). Nineteen selections are read by Ed Begley, Julie Harris, and Frederick O'Neal.

Living With Others—Citizenship I, II. Six records or tape cassettes. Society for Visual Education, Incorporated. Subjects include: Bad example of others, cheating, breaking family rules, stealing, lost friendships, safety, etc.

FILMLOOPS

Understanding Ourselves and Others. Five filmloops. Educational Reading Service. Titles: *Understanding the Difference Between Alone and Lonely; Fear — Real and Imaginary; Why We Get Angry; People Are Different, Aren't They?* and *Learning When and Where.*

Glossary

Aggression—An attempt to physically harm someone.

Anger—A defensive emotional reaction that occurs when one is frustrated, denied, or attached.

Anxiety—A feeling that exists when one is afraid but cannot recognize the cause.

Assessment—A process of collecting formal and informal data about pupils for the purpose of making instructional decisions.

Behavioral deficit—A response that presents a problem because there have been few opportunities to practice the appropriate behavior.

Behavioral description—A statement that includes a description of specific behaviors being observed.

Behavioral objective—A form for writing an instructional objective that emphasizes expected student outcomes, type of evaluation, and performance standards.

Communication—A message sent by an individual with the planned intention of affecting another individual's behavior.

Compromising—Giving up ones' goal while the other student does the same in order to reach an agreement.

Conformity—Changes in behavior that result from group influences; yielding to group pressure when no direct request has been made.

Effective communication—When a students' message is interpreted in the same way it was intended.

Fear—Real or imaginary feelings shown by students, resulting in physiological responses.

Identity—A consistent set of attitudes that describe, characterize, and define who one is.

Imaginary—Feelings or experiences that exist only in the imagination or fancy; not real experiences.

Integration—Combining several concepts, practices, approaches, methods, etc., into one idea or expression.

Intentions—Planned, deliberated, and conscious acts to satisfy immediate goals.

Internalized behavior—Intrinsic motivation that occurs when students behave appropriately because the behavior brings them personal satisfaction.

Interpersonal communication skills—Skills that promote honest communication and positive attitudes among individuals.

Modeling—A term used in social learning theory to describe how students learn as a result of observing and imitating others.

Negotiation—A process by which students who have opposite views and interests attempt to come to an agreement.

Observation—A procedure in which the observer watches and records behaviors of other individuals.

Positive reinforcement—Presenting a reward or some object that will increase positive or appropriate behaviors of pupils.

Praise—Positive verbal and nonverbal statements made by teachers to strengthen appropriate student behaviors.

Reinforcements—Rewards given for students demonstrating appropriate behaviors to increase the possibilities of those behaviors being repeated.

Rewards—Reinforcers, tangible and intangible objects, given to students to strengthen appropriate behaviors.

Self-acceptance—Pride in yourself, or a high regard for yourself.

Self-evaluation—A students' estimation of how positively his/her behaviors, manners, and actions compare with those of peers.

Social interaction—A common bond linking two or more students together.

Social skills training—A structured intervention designed to assist students in improving interpersonal skills.

Task analysis—A process for breaking down complex tasks into small manageable steps so that they can be successfully completed one at a time.

Selected Bibliography

Abell Salutes:Education Opportunity Program (EOP) at Lake Clifton-Eastern Senior High. *The Abell Report, 4,* 1, (1991).

Adams, Dennis N. (1990). Involving students in cooperative learning. *Teaching Pre K-8, 20,* 51-52.

Allen, Barbra Balfourd. (1990). *Cooperative learning workshop. Hebbville elementary school.* Baltimore, MD: Baltimore County Schools.

Anita, Shirin D. & Kreimeyer, Kathryn. (1992). *Project Interact. Interventions for social integration of young hearing-impaired children.* Washington, DC: Office of Special Education and Rehabilitative Services.

Athanases, S.Z. (1993). Adapting and tailoring lessons: Fostering teacher reflection to meet varied students' needs. *Teacher Education Quarterly, 20, 1,* 71-81.

Ayers, William. (1989). Childhood at risk. *Educational Leadership, 46,* 8:70-72.

Bandura, A. (1977). *A social learning theory.* Englewood Cliffs, NJ: Prentice-Hall.

Bandura, A. & Walters, R. (1963). *Social learning and Personality development.* New York: Holt, Rinehart and Winston.

Bank, J.A. (1991). Multicultural education: For freedom's sake. *Educational Leadership, 49,* 4:22-35.

Bankee, N.C. & Obiakor, F.E. (1992). Educating the Black male: Renewed imperatives for Black and white communities. *Scholar and Educator: The Journal of the Society of Educators and Scholars, 15,* 2:16-31.

Barth, R. (1990). *Improving schools from within.* San Francisco: Jossey-Bass, Inc.

Beane, J.A. (1990). A middle school curriculum: From Rhetoric to Reality. Columbus, OH: National Middle School Association.

Beane, James. (1993). The search for a middle school curriculum. *School Administrator, 50,* 3, 8-14.

Bennett, C. (1986). *Comprehensive multicultural education. Theory and Practice.* Boston: Allyn and Bacon.

Bert, C.R.G. & Bert, M. (1992). *The Native American: An exceptionality in education and counseling.* (ERIC Document Reproduction Service, No. Ed. 351168) Clearinghouse on Rural Education and Small Schools, Charleston, West Virginia.

Bilken, R. (1990). Making differences ordinary. In W. Stainback & M. Forest (Eds.), *Educating all children in the mainstream of regular education.* Baltimore, MD: Paul H. Brooks.

Bridges, Robert E. (1988). *Black male child development: A broken model.* Paper presented to the 120th Annual Convention, American Association of School Administrators, Las Vegas, Nevada.

Brody, Gene & Stoneman, Zolinda. (1977). *Social competencies in the developmentally disabled: Some suggestions for research and training. Mental Retardation, 15,* 4, 41-43.

Brofenbrenner, V. (1979). *The ecology of human development.* Cambridge, MA: Harvard University Press.

Brown, J. (1991, June 12). "Coleman School's All-Male Class a Success." *The Baltimore Sun,* Section D, pgs. 1,3.

Butler, Kathleen. (1988). How kids learn: What theorists say. *Learning Styles,* 30-34.

Butler, Owen B. (1989). Early help for kids at risk: Our nation's best investment. *NEA Today, 7,* 6:51-53.

Cassidy, E. (1988). Reaching and involving Black parents of handicapped children in their child's education program. Lansing, MI: Cause, Inc. (ERIC Document Reproduction Service No. Ed. 302982)

Collins, T.W. & Hatch, J.A. (1992). Supporting the social-emotional growth of young children. *Dimensions of Early Childhood, 21,* 17-21.

Committee for Economic Development. (1987). *Children in need: Investment strategies for the educationally disadvantaged.* New York.

Connolly, J. & Impura, J. (1995). *Buros' Mental Measurement Year book.* University of Nebraska Press.

Cummins, J. (1984). *Bilingual and special education: Issues in assessment pedagogy.* San Diego: College-Hill Press.

Dalli, Carmen. (1991). *Scripts for children's lives: What do parents and early childhood teachers contribute to children's understanding of events in their lives.* (ERIC Document Reproduction Service No. Ed. 344664)

Deal, Terrence E. (1990). Reforming reform. *Educational Leadership, 47,* 8:6-12.

Delgado-Gaitan, C. (1991). Involving parents in the schools: A process of empowerment. *American Journal of Education, 100,* 20-46.

DeWitt, Philip E. (1994). The crucial early years. *Time Magazine, 143,* 16, 68.

Diggory, Sylvia F. (1990). *According to schooling: The developing child.* Cambridge, MA: Harvard University Press.

DiMartino, Emily C. (1990). The remarkable social competence of young children. *International Journal of Early Childhood, 22,* 23-31.

Dodge, D.T. (1988). The creative curriculum for early childhood. Washington, DC: Creative Associates International.

Dorr-Bremme, Donald W. (1992). Discourse and social identity in a kindergarten-first grade classroom. (ERIC Document Reproduction Service No. Ed. 352111)

Eisner, E. (1991). What really counts in school? *Educational Leadership,* 10-17.

Erikson, E.H. (1959). Identity and the life cycle. *In Psychological Issues Monograph, I.* New York: International Universities Press.

Finders, Margaret & Lewis, Cynthia. (1994). Why some parents don't come to school. *Educational Leadership, 51,* 8:50-54.

Forest, M. (1990). *MAPS and cities.* Presentation at Peak Parent Center workshop, Colorado Springs, Colorado.

Foster, H.L. (1986). Jivin' and playin' the dozens. *In the persistent dilemma in our schools (2nd ed.).* Cambridge, MA: Ballinger Publishing Company.

Furnham, A. (1986). Social skills training with adolescents and young adults. In C.R. Hollins & P. Trower (Eds.), *Handbook of social skill training, 1,* 33-57. Oxford: Pergamon.

Gaeddert, W.P. (1983). "Role Model Choice: Who do women say their models are?" Detroit: *Annual Meeting of the Midwestern Psychological Association.*

Gallagher, J.J. (1989). The impact of policies for handicapped children on future early education policy. *Phi Delta Kappa,* 121-124.

Gibbs, C.R. (1991). Project 2000: Why Black men should teach Black boys. *Dollars and Sense.* February/March, 19-29.

Gibbs, Jewelle T. (1988). *Young, Black and male in America: An endangered species.* Dover, MA: Auburn House Publishing Company.

Gill, W. (1991). "Jewish Day Schools and African-American Youth." *Journal of Negro Education, 60,* 4:566-580.

Goodlad, J.L. (1984). *A Place Called School.* New York: McGraw-Hill.

Graham, P.G. (1987). "Black teachers: A drastically scarce resource." *Phi Delta Kappa, 68,* 598-605.

Gregorc, Anthony F. (1993). *An adult guide to style: The Gregorc-Style Delineator.* Columbia, CT: Gregorc Associates, Inc.

Gresham, F.M. (1985). Utility of cognitive-behavioral procedures for social skills training with children: Critical review. *Journal of Abnormal Child Psychology, 13,* 423-491.

Gresham, Frank M., and Elliott, Stephen N. (1989). Social skills deficits as a primary learning disability. *Journal of Learning Disabilities, 22,* 2:120-124.

Gruenewald, L.J. & Pollok, S.A. (1990). Language interaction in curriculum and instruction: What the classroom teacher needs to know. Austin, TX: Pro-Ed.

Haltiwanger, Jane. (1992). *A normative study of development in context: Growth toward independence in social function skills of young children.* Clearinghouse on Teacher Education. (ERIC Document Reproduction Service No. Ed. 342504) Washington, D.C.

Hamburg, David A. (1992). *A decent start: Promoting healthy child development in the first three years of life.* Clearinghouse on Teacher Education. (ERIC Document Reproduction Service No. Ed. 338431) Washington, D.C.

Harris, Shanette M. (1992). Black male masculinity and same-sex friendship. *Western Journal of Black Studies, 16,* 74-81.

Harry, B., Allen, N., & McLaughlin, M. (1992). *Communication versus compliance: Working with African-American parents in special education.* Paper presented at the Annual Meeting of the American Education Research Association, San Francisco.

Hatch, Thomas & Gardner, Howard. (1988). How kids learn: What scientists say. New research on intelligence. *Learning, 37.*

Hedley, C., Houtz, J., & Baratta, A. (1990). Cognition, curriculum, and literacy. Norwood, NJ: Ablex Publishing Company.

Hilliard, A.G. (1988). Conceptual confusion and the persistence of group oppression through education. *Journal of Equity and Excellence, 24,* 1:36-43.

Hilliard, A.G. (1989). Teachers and cultural styles in a pluralistic society. *NEA Today, 7,* 6:65-69.

Holland, Spencer. (1987). A radical approach to educating young Black males. *Education Week,* Commentary, 24-25.

Holland, Spencer. (1991). *Why Black men should teach Black boys. Project 2000.* Baltimore, MD: A report submitted to the Baltimore City Public Schools.

Holland, Spencer H. (1992). Same gender classes in Baltimore: How to avoid problems faced in Detroit, Milwaukee. *Journal of Equity and Excellence, 25,* 2-4, 93.

Hudley, Cynthia A. (1992). *The reduction of peer directed aggression among highly aggressive African-American boys.* Clearinghouse on Teacher Education. (ERIC Document Reproduction Service No. Ed. 346204) Washington, D.C.

Hudley, Cynthia A. (1993). An attributional intervention to reduce peer-directed aggression among African-American boys. *Child Development, 64,* 124-138.

Ingrassia, M. (1993). "Endangered Family." *Newsweek, 122,* 17-29.

Irvine, J.J. (1989). "Beyond Role Models: An Examination of Cultural Influences on the Pedagogical Perspectives of Black Teachers." *Peabody Journal of Education, 66,* 4:218-226.

Jewett, Jan. (1992). *Aggression and cooperation: Helping young children develop constructive strategies.* Clearinghouse on Teacher Education. (ERIC Document Reproduction Service No. Ed. 351147)

Johnson, D.W., Johnson, R., & Holubec, E. (1988). *Cooperation in the classroom.* Edina, MN: Interaction Book Company.

Johnson, W., & Johnson, R. (1990). Social skills for successful group work. *Educational Leadership, 47,* 4:29-33.

Kagan, S.L. (1989). Early care and education: Beyond the schoolhouse doors. *Phi Delta Kappa,* 107-112.

Kagan, Spencer. (1990). The structural approach to cooperative learning. *Educational Leadership, 47,* 4:12-15.

Katz, L.G. (1991). The teacher's role in social development of young children. Urbana, Illinois Clearinghouse on Elementary and Early Childhood Education (ERIC Document Reproduction Service No. Ed. 331642)

Kristo, J.V. & Heath, P.A. (1982). Today's curriculum: An integrative approach. Washington, DC: University of America Press.

Lane, Pamela S. & McWhirter, J.J. (1992). A peer mediation model: Conflict resolution for elementary and middle school children. *Elementary School Guidance & Counseling, 27,* 15-21.

LaPoint, V. (1992). "Accepting Community Responsibility for African American Youth Education and Socialization." *Journal of Negro Education, 61,* 4:451-454.

Lareau, A. (1987). Social class differences in family school relationships: The importance of cultural capital. *Sociology of Education, 60,* 73-85.

Lutfiyya, Z. (1988). *Reflections and relationships between people with disabilities and typical people.* Syracuse, NY: Syracuse University, Center on Human Policy.

Lutfiyya, Z. (1991). *Tony Santi and the bakery: The roles of facilitation, accommodation, and interpretation.* Syracuse, NY: Syracuse University, Center on Human Policy.

Lynch, E.W., & Stein, R. (1987). Parent participation by ethnicity: A comparison of Hispanic, Black, and Anglo families. *Exceptional Children, 54,* 105-111.

Mancus, S.M. (1992). "Influence of male teachers on elementary school children's stereotyping of teacher competence." *Sex Roles, 26,* 3:109-126.

Mansbach, S.C. (1993). We must put family literacy on the national agenda. *Reading Today, 37.*

Marion, R. (1981). *Educators, parents and exceptional children.* Rockville, MD: Aspen.

Matsueda, R.L. & Heimer, K. (1987). Race, family, structure, and delinquency: A test differential association and social control theories. *American Sociological Review, 54,* 6:826-840.

McGinnis, E. & Goldstein, A. (1984). *Skill streaming the elementary child.* IL: Research Press Company.

McRae, Larry. (1994). The need for African-American male teachers as role models. Unpublished Master's Thesis: Coppin State College.

Moll, Ian. (1991). *The material and to social in Vygotsky's theory of cognitive development.* Clearinghouse on Teacher Education. (ERIC Document Reproduction Service No. Ed. 346988) Washington, D.C.

Obiakor, F.E. (1990). Development of self-concept: Impact on students' learning. *The Journal of the Southeastern Association of Educational Opportunity Program Personnel, 9,* 1:16-23.

Obiakor, F.E. (1991). Self-concept: Impact on Black students' learning. *SENGA, 1,* 2:48:53.

Obiakor, F.E. (1992). Self-concept of African-American students: An operational model for special education. *Exceptional Children, 59,* 2:160-167.

O'Brien, J. & O'Brien, C. (1991). *Members of each other-perspectives on social support for people with severe disabilities.* Lithuania, GA: Responsive Systems Associates.

O'Brien, L. (1989). Learning styles make the student aware. *NASSP Bulletin,* October, 85-89.

Odom, S. & McEvoy, M. (1988). Integration of young children with handicapped and non-handicapped children: Mainstreamed versus integrated special education. In S. Odom & M. Karnes (Eds.), *Early Intervention for Infants and Children with Handicaps: An Empirical Base,* (pp. 241-267). Baltimore, MD: Paul H. Brooks.

Oswald, Donald P. & Sinah-Nirbay, N. (1992). Current research on social behavior. *Behavior Modification, 16,* 4:443-447.

Owens, S.J. (1991). Establishing staff training for identifying learning styles in the preschool setting. (ERIC Document Reproduction Service No. Ed. 342501)

Peck, C.A. & Cooke, T.P. (1983). Benefits of mainstreaming at the early childhood level: How much can we expect? *Analysis and intervention in developmental disabilities, 3,* 1-22.

Poplin, M.S. (1988). Holistic/constructivist principles of the teaching/learning process: Implications for the field of learning disabilities. *Journal of Learning Disabilities, 21,* 7:410-416.

Project 2000 Teacher Assistant Orientation. Center for educating African-American males. School of Education and Urban Studies, Morgan State University, Baltimore, MD.

Rancifer, J.L. (1991). "Restructuring teacher education: Effective strategies to increase the number of Black students in education programs." Association of Teacher Educators, Washington, D.C.

Reynolds, J., et al. (1992). Learning style characteristics: An introductory workshop. Clearinghouse on Teacher Education, 66, 2:122-126.

Rizzo, J.V. & Zabel, R.H. (1988). *Educating children and adolescents with behavioral disorders: An integrative approach.* Boston: Allyn and Bacon, Inc.

Ross, D.D., Bundy, E. & Kyle, D.W. (1993). Reflective teaching for student empowerment. New York, NY: MacMillan.

Salend, Spencer J. & Whittaker, C.R. (1992). Group evaluation: A collaborative, peer-mediated behavior management system. *Exceptional Children, 59,* 203-209.

Schultz, J.L. (1990). Cooperative learning: The first year. *Educational Leadership, 47,* 4:43-45.

Shade, B.J. & Edward, P. (1987). "Ecological Correlation of the Educative Style of African-American Children." *Journal of Negro Education, 56,* 1:88-89.

Shade, B.J. (1989). The influence of perceptual development on cognitive style: Cross ethnic comparison. *Early Child Development and Care, 51,* 137-155.

Slavin, R. (1991). *Using student team learning.* Baltimore, MD: Johns Hopkins University, The Centre for Social Organization of Schools.

Slavin, R.E. & Oickle, E. (1981). Effects of cooperative learning teams on student achievement and race relations: Treatment by race interactions. *Sociology of Education, 54,* 174-180.

Sloan, T.L. (1992). "Influence of male teachers on elementary school children." *Sex Roles, 26,* 4:120-126.

Smith, V.E. (1993). Three reasons to keep "hustling," pg. 22. (In Ingrassia, *Endangered Family, Newsweek, 122,* 1993).

Smith, V.E. (1993). Two dads and a dream—but not illusions. *Newsweek, 122,* 21. (In Ingrassia, *Endangered Family, Newsweek, 122,* 1993).

Stewart, J., Meier, K., England, R. (1989). "In quest of role models: Change in Black teacher representation in urban school districts, 1968-1986." *Journal of Negro Education, 58,* 2:140-152.

Stuart, Richard B. (1989). Social learning theory: A vanishing or expanding presence? *Psychology: A Journal of Human Behavior, 26,* 1:35-50.

Taylor, George. (1992). Impact of social learning theory on educating deprived/minority children. Clearinghouse for Teacher Education. (ERIC Document Reproduction Service No. Ed. 349260) Washington, D.C.

Taylor, George. (1993). *Black male project. Report submitted to Sinclair Lane Elementary School.* Baltimore, MD.

Taylor, George. (1994). Three evaluation reports on evaluating social skills of young African-American males. Reports submitted to Sinclair Lane Elementary School, Baltimore, MD.

Tharp, R.G. (1989). Psychocultural variables and constraints: Effects on teaching and learning in schools. *American Psychologist, 44,* 2:349-359.

The National Association of State Boards of Education. (1992). Alexandria, VA: Author.

Thomas, Pierre. (1995). One in 3 young Black men in the justice system. *The Washington Post,* October 5.

Tomlinson, Sally. (1988). Why Johnny can't read: Critical theory and special education. *European Journal of Special Needs Education, 3,* 45-58.

Vasquez, J.A. (1991). *Cognitive style and academic achievement in cultural diversity and the schools: Consensus and controversy.* (Edited by J. Lynch, C. Modgil, ad S. Modgil). London: Falconer Press.

Vincent, J.P. (1990). *The Biology of Emotions.* Cambridge, MA: Basil Blackwell.

Vygotsky, L.S. (use Moll, IBN 1991). *The material and the social.* Series on cognitive development. Clearinghouse on Teacher Education (ED. 352186).

Wake County Public School System. (1989). School/community helping hands project: A plan to combat negative influences on Black male youth. Raleigh, NC.

Walker, Hill M., Irvin, Larry K, Noell, John & Singer, George H.S. (1992). A construct score approach to the assessment of social competence. *Behavior Modification, 16,* 4:449-452.

Wiley, R. (1991). "Why Black people tend to shout." *Carroll Publishing Group*. Washington, DC.

Witken, H. (1973). Some implications of research on cognitive style and problems for education. In personality and learning: Hood and Stoughton.

Wood, J.W. (1984). *Adapting instruction for the mainstream*. Columbus, OH: Charles E. Merrill.

Wright, Willie J. (1992). The endangered Black male child. *Educational Leadership, 49,* 4:14-17.

Index

About the Author

GEORGE R. TAYLOR is Professor of Special Education and Chairperson of the Department of Special Education at Coppin State College in Baltimore, Maryland and a Core Faculty Member of the Union Institute in Cincinnati, Ohio. Dr. Taylor has authored or contributed to three textbooks and over 15 articles on trends and issues in education.

MAI

5-20-98

GAYLORD F

ISBN 0-275-95200-2

90000>

EAN

9 780275 952006

HARDCOVER BAR CODE